Dynamic Aging

I Intend To Live Forever,

So Far So Good!

Joy Sloan Jinks

NOWTIME Publications
YOUR WORDS YOUR WAY

P.O. Box 126
Cottonwood, AL 3632
nowtimepublications@gmail.com

DEDICATION

To my husband of 60 plus years, who at 92, is a Miller County Commissioner, a Philanthropist, Church Treasurer, and Choir Member, the model of a man who has aged dynamically while driving around town in his 1984 truck. His love and support of my endeavors have made it all possible.

ACKNOWLEDGEMENTS

My thanks to the people who did not laugh when I said I was going to write a book:

Jean Houston and Peggy Rubin, remarkable women of intellect and heart, who taught me to play in the field of possibilities;

My sister, Betty Miller, who gave me a bookmark that quoted James Barrie, "It is all well and good to write books, but can you wiggle your ears?" I can't wiggle my ears but she can;

My friend and colleague, Karen Kimbrel, with whom I have shared "many brilliant ideas of the day" during the early years of Swamp Gravy;

The creative people of Colquitt, and southwest Georgia, whose 'can do' spirit has created a destination city in this town of 2,000, where the arts are performed and celebrated;

The remarkable people who find their way to Colquitt, GA, each January to participate in the Building Creative Communities Conference to celebrate together the power of coming together to co-create a world that works for everyone;

And, lastly, the team who helped to birth this book, and who found me through the working of the Spirit in our lives:

- Jennifer Bradford, creative designer, computer whiz and Girl Friday;
- Audri Scott Williams, my editor, a woman of amazing talent and experience whose dedication to social justice and peace brings light to dark places;
- Trish Broersma, the graphic designer who brought the cover of the book ALIVE!

Eternal gratitude to all of you.

CONTENTS

FORWARD

Springy red hair, startling blue eyes, southern drawl that brooks no whiny nay saying, Joy Jinks is a revelation to all who meet her. Looking and acting ageless, she is the epitome of what seniors could and should be. Rightly named Joy, there is little or no negativity in her. Like the happy warrior that she is, she finds what needs to be done and then goes about and does it. When her town of Colquitt, Georgia was suffering from economic and racial tensions, she created, with the brilliant partnership of theater director Richard Geer, a new concept in social theater in which the residents of the town told their stories, resolved their hurts, and learned how the ones they had feared were their most trusted allies.

She had previously brought new life and economics into the town by creating businesses, modeling good citizenship, and being a very good friend to all she encountered.

Now in this magnificent book, she brings the essence of her life's experience into wildly original ideas and stories. Here are gems to inspire, questions to evoke one's higher nature, and exercises to bring one to new ways of being and understanding. After reading this marvel of a woman's soul, I have decided that I want to be Joy Jinks when I grow up!

Joy addresses the dynamics of aging beautifully and gives us the great gift of renewing our options, as we become sages and discover that with the breadth of life behind one, the depths are now at hand. The time of our realized maturity, what we are calling the Sage years, from 65 to 100, is the inheritor of this breadth and the bearer of these depths. For many of us, our years are being extended as our options and opportunities are being increased. We now have the time to become who we are; no longer men and women working a few short years in search of subsistence. Rather, we now are gaining a life span that allows us to become sages, richly actualized human beings able to transcend the particularities of our local selves, able to deal wisely and creatively with the enormous personal and planetary complexities of our time.

We are gradually coming to see that the years beyond sixty five or seventy, the years of our second maturity, may be evolution's greatest gift to humanity. Relieved of the armoring of authority of one's first maturity, as well as its accompanying narrowing of vision, one gains in these years the liberty to inquire rather than order, to question rather than reply. No longer encapsulated by ends and goals, delivered   from specialized commitments, the old are free to explore the fullness of their psychophysical powers, the latencies of their human potentials. New ways are emerging in which we can reset the cellular aging clock and thus send senescence on its way to obsolescence.

Our Sages are the harbingers of the possible human. What we already are, if we would but become, are beings who can be both uniquely ourselves and members of a group, in community, as knowing wise carriers of both inner and outer ecologies. We are capable of marrying the integral depths of the self, with its rich matrix of forms, to the analytic observations of existential life. When this happens, then creative thinking and imaginative and efficient problem solving become the normal way of life, making the extraordinary the ordinary and natural way of being. Then the cooperative flow between ourselves and others will also become natural, replacing the competition and violence that stand in attendance upon our present limited and limiting selves. The great forms of union, whether religious, sexual, or aesthetic — or the communion that occurs in the genius of friendship — will become for the many the modes of evolutionary transformation. The key to all this is the genius inherent in dynamic aging, and in the mind and heart of Joy Jinks we are given the finest realization of the ways to accomplish this and more.

Read this book. Give it to your friends. Shout about it from the roof tops. And, above all, practice its principles and see how your life and your world will change.

Jean Houston

INTRODUCTION

"I INTEND TO LIVE FOREVER,
SO FAR SO GOOD."

"I was growing old while waiting for my wrinkle cream to work." A television ad for Neutrogena.

One morning I woke up and realized that I was approaching my 80th birthday. I had the feeling that others have expressed, "How did this happen, when did this happen and what happened?" At the same time I was struck with wonder and amazement at my life as I remembered many different crooks and turns and opportunities that were due to chance meetings and feelings of being in the "flow." I was grateful for the doors that opened when I thought there were no doors, the people who mentored me when I was a confused adolescent and the family who loved and supported me through it all.

I was in a retrospective mood, not just because people kept urging me to write my story, but I was trying to figure out why I felt like I was at the "top of my game" at 80 years old. Even though I was troubled by some aches and pains, my health was good and my excitement about life had not diminished. I was a housewife in the 1950's, a wife and a mother of three, gotten my Master's degree in Social Work at age 40, had a career, been an entrepreneur, a community organizer, an international volunteer and a community arts consultant.

I started looking at my life with questions, such as: "What are the personal beliefs, major influences and daily practices that have brought me to this place and continue to sustain me at this time?" Over a lifetime many people and learning experiences helped shape my perspectives. The major influences are: my upbringing in the Methodist church which set me on a spiritual path and fostered in me the desire to be of service; my volunteer work with the Institute of Cultural Affairs which opened up the world to me; and my years of study with Dr. Jean Houston, whose intellect ranks with the greatest of our time.

These influences created in me the desire to know more and to grow deeper. At a Jean Houston symposium in 1990, I met a theater director named Dr. Richard Geer and we became co-founders of Swamp Gravy, Georgia's folk life play, which in over 20 years, has revitalized a rural town and been a pioneer in economic development through the Arts and Culture.

This book offers a journey, exploration using yourself as a research subject to embrace strategies that will lead to a richer, fuller life in the years after retirement.

If you are reading this, you are probably a Baby Boomer, the name given to those born between 1946 and 1964 and who now make up 40% of the population, or roughly 76 million people. You may be a child of the "Greatest Generation" because your parents grew up during the depression and became the heroes of World War ll. In addition, many of them, not away at war, had a decisive economic impact on our country during the war.

As a member of the Boomer generation, you are facing retirement and may be curious about this very different stage of life and seeking to determine ways to create a life after work. Perhaps the greatest contribution of the Boomer generation will be to create a new model of what it means to live as a dynamic elder.

The realization that ten thousand people retire every day is staggering. People who are above one hundred are the fastest growing segment of society. The implications for health care, recreation, housing, Social Security and Medicare are mind-boggling. Futurists are trying to project possible solutions to the demands these changes will bring. Those who are living these dramatic changes can resolve to be involved in the dialogue and offer experience-based wisdom to move us to the next point of discussion: individually; as social group; and, as a society.

We are bombarded by messages about how to live longer and look younger - the right vitamins to take; the right diet; exercise; even make-up and plastic surgery. Women's magazines have articles about looking young after 30, looking glamorous in your 40s, being sexy in your 50s. How about sex after 50, or 60 or 70 or 80? Is the apex of life at 40 and it's all downhill from there?

Finally, as important as exercise and nutrition are, the challenge to aging dynamically is to maintain attitudes of mind and heart that can invigorate us so that we can be fully engaged no matter how old we are.

The present attitudes toward aging in our country are negative. Ram Dass says that, "…aging is a great social ill and remains one of our cultures last taboos. He reiterates that elders are seen as silly, stubborn, vindictive, or worst of all, cute."

Sue Balducci thinks that old age comes at a bad time. Just when we think we might understand something about life we are faced with retirement, loss of status in the working world, declining energy and possible loss of a partner. Elders are immediately put in a box labeled feeble, decrepit, senile, a drain on society.

Younger family and friends watch for signs of memory slippage, decline in alertness, slowing down of gait or other signs of mental and physical decline. Many people hesitate to tell their age because they believe that they will be treated differently. Some even refuse to tell their age when asked how old they are and retort, "I'm as old as dirt, what's it to you." However, in most societies in the world, the elders are treated with respect, honored for their wisdom and life experience and children are taught that the aged ones are special and their presence in the family home is welcomed.

At every transition point in life we have the recurrent dilemma of figuring out our role all over again. We have learned to recreate ourselves at each developmental stage of life: i.e. childhood, teenager, young adult, parent, career, retirement, and beyond. Can you remember the challenges of going from childhood to pre-teen, then teen years, adulthood, career, possibly marriage and parenting? As we recall these times, we realize how much we have learned along the way that can be applied to the next development stage which Leif Erickson calls "generativity versus stagnation." Erickson defines generativity as the time of giving back, helping, contributing to the welfare of the world.

If, indeed, as social scientists predict, we are going to be living much longer lives, it behooves us to model a new way of being that will change the present paradigm on aging. The generation of the Baby Boomers has the challenge and the opportunity to create new input that will impact present and future attitudes toward aging.

In the final analysis this book is about empowerment. Empowerment is defined by the United Nations

Department of Economic and Social Affairs (UNDESA), as a "long term process affected by and resulting in changes in norms, values, rules, institutions and social relations." As this generation of new retirees determines to look squarely into the face of the present paradigm, see its flaws, its limiting belief systems, its prejudices, we can begin to ask the questions and challenge the assumptions and demonstrate a new way of living.

If empowerment is a long term process about changes in norms, the norms around aging presently have to do with viewing the time after retirement as a downhill slide into boredom, ill health, and depression. The new norm can be seen as a time to move from "old" to "new", new interests, new expectations, and the most creative, fulfilling time of life.

Many times, elderly are seen as a drain on society's

limited health care resources. The change in values will be seen as elders are valued for their wisdom and contributions to the ongoing pageant of human life. While whole categories of people are recognized and honored, for instance, veterans, union organizers, suffragettes, civil rights activists, etc. many times, ordinary people are not acknowledged by family or younger acquaintances for their sacrifice and hard work.

As mature adults, we have witnessed the breakdown of all the major systems that govern our society and impinge upon our lives. In this time of "whole systems transition," retirees have the time and intellectual resources to make valuable contributions to the creation of new institutions and systems of care. What are the changes in institutions such as the retirement, education, social security and health care systems that need to be part of this dialogue? Should rules related to retirement at age 65 be changed so that the elderly are no longer perceived as a drain but a contributor to the safety net systems? What new societal roles and ways to contribute are waiting to be modeled?

What are the changes in social roles that will be tools of empowerment? In the 1985 movie, "Trip to Bountiful," an elderly Texas woman has one burning desire: to go on a sentimental journey to Bountiful, the little town of her childhood home. She lives with her hateful daughter-in-law and her weak son and has to hide her social security check from her controlling family. Her low self-esteem and her lack of self-determination are, many times, the story of growing old. But the time is fast approaching when agency is restored to those who are retired, because we demand it. The goal of this book is the empowerment of elders from silent and powerless to playing important roles in building a future for our grand children and great grandchildren.

Boomers are the generation who can pioneer a new way of experiencing the latter years. What is the new story about aging that needs to be lived, rehearsed and written large? I invite you to be part of the grand experiment, to read this book attentively, and relate its poetry, stories and suggestions to your own life experiences. I challenge you to experience life as an adventure, to expand your body's sensory awareness, and to become ecstatic by the beauty and wonder of the journey. But more than that, I challenge you to become empowered as you journey through this book, and to use your newly recognized abilities to impact the pain, the injustice, and the heartbreak of the world. In the process, we can grow our heart like the tin man, call forth the courage of the cowardly lion, and rewire the brain neurons like the scarecrow.

This book is a beginning. The psycho-spiritual practices that are offered in the following chapters can be a grand experiment in soul work for those approaching these most rewarding and challenging years. After all:

- To Pay Attention brings Aliveness
- Aliveness allows us to accept Challenges
- Challenges lead to Adventure
- Adventure means Fun
- Having fun is Play
- Play gives opportunities to Converse
- In Conversing we Unpack our stories
- Unpacking leads to Celebrate
- Celebration is a way to Give Back
- Giving back brings Joy
- Attitude beacons us to pay attention
- Joy calls forth Gratitude.

The purposes of this book are: to foster the spiritual disciplines that help us navigate this demanding time of life; to begin the dialogue to change the present paradigm about aging; and to empower the reader to become the activist that uses their wisdom, skills, time and talents to create the new social systems for our children and grandchildren.

So have fun with this and let's talk about our experiences. See my website and send me your thoughts: www.dynamicaging.net

Mad Woman of Chailott

Of course in the morning it does not always feel so gay. Not when you are taking your hair out of the dresser and your teeth out of the glass. And particularly, if you've been dreaming that you are a little girl on a pony looking for strawberries in the woods. But then comes a letter in the morning mail. One you wrote yourself, giving your schedule for the day …

Then, when I have washed in rosewater and put on my pins, rings, brooches, pearls, necklaces, I'm ready to begin again."

"After that, everything is pure delight." It is time for me to dress for my morning walk. Then I begin my rounds, I walk toward the Square, blowing kisses to each friend. I have my cats to feed, my dogs to pet, my plants to water. So how does life seem now?

To be alive is very fortunate.

Jean Giraudorex, 1942

CHAPTER ONE

ATTITUDE

"From Ho-Hum to Wow"

Jean Giraudorex has shown us a word picture in his play, *Mad Woman of Chaillot,* of an attitude toward life that one would do well to emulate. The so called "mad woman," embraces life in spite of her status as an elder, even as she takes her "hair out of the drawer" and her "teeth out of the glass." She enjoys the memories of the happy times of her childhood without a hint of sadness or depression. She plans her day so that she has reason to get out of bed and has something to look forward to even as she embraces life in all its brokenness. She takes what life has handed her and makes the best of it.

She uses the resources that she has to look her very best and create the persona that she wants to project to the world. She cares for those who are dependent on her, her beloved animals. Only then is she ready to begin her day and becomes queen of her own life, the star of her own drama. What a picture she paints of spreading joy by loving her pets and throwing kisses to all her admirers!

Finally, she is filled with gratitude. "To be alive is very fortunate." Jean Giraudorex.

One can learn a lot from this madwoman who seems very sane.

Any discussion of aging begins with the exploration of our attitude toward the years after retirement. Is your attitude positive or negative, hopeful or dread-filled? It is worth examining our attitude, since our attitude determines our outlook, our energy level, and the people that we attract into our life.

After all, how old is old? As my doctor says you are as old as your mind tells your body, you are as old as you think you are. He believes that your attitude can make you old or keep you more youthful. The study of the influence of our mind on our body has opened up a growing field of exploration called Mind/Body medicine. More and more scientific studies point to the importance of our thoughts in determining our health. As the adage says, "Your body believes every word you say." As we focus on the true, the beautiful and the good, neural path ways are flooded with feel good hormones and we are happier and more youthful.

Unless we choose our attitude toward aging it is likely to be determined by society's cultural expectations and our own pre-conceived ideas. Our attitude toward growing older can be influenced by many things such as our family view on aging, our health and our personality type. Our understanding of our genetic heritage can determine whether we think we will die at 60 or live to be 100. Also the expectation that we will grow old and infirm at a certain age can create a sense of hopelessness and reinforce negative perceptions. Ask yourself who in your family might have influenced your attitude toward growing old.

It can be helpful during the retirement years to have a role model for aging dynamically. My role model has been my Aunt, my Father's sister, who lived to be a hardy and robust 87. I heard stories about her all my life. She graduated from a high school in the north Georgia mountains about the time of the First World War. She went to work in a Doctor's office and helped send my Father to college in the 1920s. In 1923 she "bobbed" her hair, she started smoking, she bought her first car and she went to New York for the first time! She was the first liberated woman in our family and never lost her sense of adventure, her self-reliance and her strong will. She lived for a time in Okinawa, where her husband was an engineer and bought beautiful hand crafts native to the culture.. She lived dynamically until she died and demonstrated that the way one ages is a continuation of the way one has lived. What stories do you remember about a relative who influenced your attitude about living as a dynamic elder?

The status of our health certainly influences our attitude toward all of life. Do you make a conscious effort to take care of your body or do you ignore the warning signs and think you can beat the odds if you abuse your body? Are you a closet hypochondriac? The old joke "I told you I was sick," can become a self-fulfilling prophesy.

Our attitude is also influenced by the type of personality we are born with and the experiences that reinforced our early beliefs about life. Our attitude colors every experience we have since we take our own atmosphere with us. Just think of Joe Btfspik, the character in Al Capp's satirical comic strip who always had a dark cloud hanging over his head and felt that he always had bad luck. The people who whistle while they work attract us into their circle of happiness while those born with a more morose personality can be hard to be around and easy to ignore.

Even though many factors help to determine our basic attitude toward aging and toward life, attitude in any situation is a choice. Attitude can be a mental outlook or a mind-set or a point of view but in reality it is based in habit. Practices become habituated because they serve our ego's goals. For example, we let depression rule us because of our desire for sympathy, to be taken care of, or to have those we love cater to our needs. In this way we wallow in self-pity, and inward feelings of doubt and distress. We can change our habits by changing our thinking and thereby change our attitudes.

Victor Frankl believed that "everything can be taken from a man but one thing; the last of the human freedoms-to choose one's attitude in any given set of circumstances, to choose one's own way". Frankl was sorely tested during the years he spent in the fire of a Nazi concentration camp and wrote about his experiences in his seminal work "Man's Search for Meaning." Can you imagine waking up every morning in the horror of a death camp and realizing that all you had was the ability to choose the way you would respond to what was happening all around?

In that severe environment where the horror accompanying life and death was omnipresent, Frankl, a psychiatrist who had specialized in suicide, discovered that the freedom to choose one's attitude always remained. He postulates that when bad things happen, we have three choices: to let bad things define us, destroy us or strengthen us. The truth about life comes down to our attitude. It is all in our choice of attitude.

If we change our attitude we can change our lives. Boomers can change their attitude and hereby change the present world view about getting "old." The Baby Boomer generation is the first generation in history to have the luxury of a long life after retirement. It is their responsibility, and challenge, to create a new way of thinking and being, to grow depth to harvest the richness of their lives and co-create and communicate a new way of being.

What are the attitudes that we need to cultivate and bring into this time of life? Perhaps the most important is the acceptance of life as it has unfolded. Life seldom goes according to the plans and dreams we had when we were young. In the movie, "Les Miserable," as Fontine is dying, she sings the poignant,

"I dreamed a dream in days gone by," expressing the angst of a⸱ ᴜnfulfilled life. And as Forest Gump reminds, ⸱⸱ᴇ a box of chocolates, you never know wha⸱ ɢet."

Grievinɡ a necessary step toward ⸱s been given us. Harbᴄ ⸱nd that has been dealt ⸱ssion, while being angry ⸱s futile. When we remiɴ⸱ ⸱ɴaᴛ ᴛnings have a way of working out," we ᴄ⸱ ᴋe a long view and not get caught up in moment-by-moment worries and frustrations.

The acceptance of our own foibles, mistakes, unskilled behaviors, (called sins in some religious traditions), and mess-ups, is another part of accepting the journey of our life. It is freeing to acknowledge the fact that we are capable of committing any dastardly act that anyone else has ever been guilty of doing. In this knowledge, we can accept ourselves as well as our fellow human beings, warts, beauty, and all. As we forgive ourselves and those who have wounded us, we can move on to a happier life. The acceptance of the Mystery of Life, in all its glory and pain, can give us a sense of our place in the long march of humanity.

Why are we here in this galaxy, in this far corner of the Milky Way? Is this *God School*, a place for us to look deeply into our meaning and purpose, and ask ourselves the hard questions in preparation for sharing our mind and heart for the good of the planet?

Are we, perhaps, here to learn and to pass on to others, by our example and our words, the wisdom we have garnered?

In the midst of all the mayhem our news media feeds

us every day, how do we create and maintain a positive attitude? I am suggesting a few simple practices that may help keep our attitude positive. Every day may not be a high but every day can be one of a good outlook.

As we surround ourselves with positive people, those who fill our cups and we fill theirs, we can stay on a happy wavelength and "Don't let the turkeys get us down." The fastest way to change a good day into a not so good day is to be around negative, complaining people. The energy vampires will suck the life and joy out of us if they have a chance. Let us be on guard to protect your "head and heart space" from those who can only deplete you. Negative people can create an energy field called by noted biologist, Rupert Sheldrake, a morphogenetic field, which affects our mood.

Likewise a "love feast' with friends creates a

morphogenetic field which fills us with joy. Laughter is the key to change the morphogenetic field from gloom to satisfaction and pleasure.

At times we are our own worst enemy. When we allow the inner critic to find fault, it becomes one of the greatest robbers of our joy and self-confidence. I had an experience of the inner critic, last summer, when my almost 15 year old granddaughter was visiting. I had a new car, and I was getting used to a different set of bells and whistles. This child, who was not old enough to have a learner's permit, started criticizing my driving.

Suddenly, I found myself doubting my ability to drive safely, even though my last accident was 20 years ago and was not my fault. I learned very quickly how even unfounded criticism can influence the inner critic and under mind self-confidence.

The great news of current brain research shows the neuroplasticity of the brain which means that your brain does not stop growing at a certain age, but continues to change and make connections between cells. If you can change your mind, you can change your life. We don't have to decline in mental capacities, but can continue to grow new brain cells, neurons and synapses. When we get out of our rut, have new experiences, make new friends, and learn new things, our brains grow. As we nourish positive interactions, the neural pathways are flooded with "feel good" hormones and we are happier.

A creative hobby can forge new neural pathways in the brain and can open the doors to new friends. Hobbies are a way to channel physical and psychic energy into positive pursuits. Many people have returned to their love of making music in their later years and have brought back youthful memories, renewing high school friendships through reunions of groups long disbanded.

My friend, Dot, who has not had an easy life, is in her early 80's. She finds herself with back problems that are almost debilitating. But Dot has never been one to give in to her feelings. She is a volunteer extraordinaire and is planning three major fund raisers for our local Arts Council. She has created a line of greeting cards using pressed flowers from her garden and takes online classes to increase her skill. She is a prime example of a woman who has re-invented herself over and over. Her wonderful attitude toward life and what is possible, even in the midst of pain, is inspiring to all who know her.

In addition, the practice of small acts of kindness, whether random or by design, can change our day from the usual to memorable. Such simple things as telling the young waitress or cashier how pretty she is, or playing peek-a-boo with a baby or sending a card to a shut-in, fills our hearts and our brains with feel-good hormones. If, before falling asleep, we count the acts of kindness we have shown, we will, perhaps, find that the number of kindnesses is the same as the number of blessings we have received.

Baby Boomers find themselves at a juncture in their own lives and in the life of the culture. As they face retirement and a new focus, they can turn their attention to their own attitudes toward aging, as well as noticing how current society views elderly people. Taking a lesson from The Mad Woman of Chaillot, we can face each day with the attitude, "To be alive is very fortunate."

Go Deeper

A poem was popular a few years ago entitled *"When I am old I shall wear purple."* Women of a certain age started to join the Purple Hat society. Membership in this club announced to the world that age was to be celebrated.

Let us look in our toy box of crayons and put on our purple hats and think about the following:

○ How old would you be if your birth certificate had been lost and you had no idea when you were born?

○ Do you hate the idea of retirement? Do you feel that the most productive time of your life is over or are you looking forward to the time when you can re-create yourself? What is your heart's desire to do when you are not tied down?

o Who is your role model for growing older?

Go Lighter

o For fun, do a brain dump of everything that is the color purple. Start with "purple people eaters."

o What is the zaniest thing you can imagine yourself doing? What is the most fun thing you can imagine yourself doing to celebrate your attitude toward aging?

o Choose one of the above and *Just Do It !*o In honor of the symbol of the color purple send a card or a gift to a person who represents, for you, a beautiful attitude toward aging.

o Celebrate your age by singing "Happy Birthday to Me".

What a Gift

What a gift to have lived in you, body...
Seeing through your eyes
Dancing with your feet
Breathing from your lungs
Talking with your voice
Hugging with your arms.

And sensing with your spirit
Bright blessed day
Love of my kin and
Our common Earth.

What a gift it is
To live in you, body
Thanks for carrying me
So long, so far,
And oh so well

Most of all, thanks for putting me
In touch with spirit
At the heart of it all.

John Cock

CHAPTER TWO

PAY ATTENTION

"Old Age is Not a Disease"

The first step toward aging with vitality and verve is possibly just to "pay attention" or simply to be *aware*. Spiritual teachers often say, "Wake Up."

The primary object of attention is what our body perceives through the five senses. Sensory data are bombarding us in every moment, but to really experience what our senses are telling us we need to pay attention.

Sometimes daily life is on automatic pilot, and routine can be the most comfortable place. The psyche can become encrusted with sameness, same emotions, same expectations, responses and prejudices. The senses become dull and life becomes jaded. We no longer feel the excitement of Christmas or a special celebration. We take everything for granted and become bored. Bored people are generally boring people. But we do not have to settle into the rut of boredom and perhaps pettiness. In these transition years into older adulthood (from 55-85) we can determine to become more and more alive. Paying attention to our senses is the first step.

In fact, there is nothing stopping us from experiencing our senses afresh, the way we did as small children. John Cock's poem, "What a gift it is to have lived in you, body," reminds us of the blessings our senses are. Our bodies are wonderfully made and we take it all for granted. Helen Keller is revered because she lived such a rich, full life even though she was denied the ability to see and hear. Yet she used her sense of touch to connect with the world and even to learn to talk and read. She became an icon for what a human can accomplish even in the midst of great challenges.

"Use your eyes as if tomorrow you would be stricken blind. Hear the music of voices, the song of birds; the mighty strain of an orchestra, as if you would be stricken deaf tomorrow. Touch each object as if your tactile sense would fail. Smell the perfume of flowers, taste with relish each morsel, as if tomorrow you could never smell and taste again. Make the most of every sense; glory in all the facets of pleasure and beauty which the world reveals to you." (Helen Keller)

What a feast for the senses is afforded us if we only pay attention to the data our senses bring us. We can almost taste the happiness such experiences allow us.

My favorite place to pay attention to my senses is the beach. Join with me in your imagination as I watch the sunset on the Gulf Coast near Panama City Beach, Florida. The sand, as soft and white as sugar, is cool to my feet and pulls on every muscle in my legs as I walk. The sky is a glorious combination of every shade of pink and magenta. The sun, within 10 minutes of setting, is leaving a path of golden light from the white sand of the beach across the water to the horizon. The sky is covered by wispy clouds that are so brightly colored that I feel like I am walking in a rainbow. The weather is a little stormy so the sound of the waves is louder than usual and the smell of the salt spray is invigorating. Such beauty makes me feel like I am standing on tiptoe in wonder and amazement.

Traditionally, the five physical senses, sight, taste, touch, hearing and smell have been acknowledged as the primary ways to learn and to relate to the world around us. How many senses are you aware of as you read these words? Are you sitting in a comfortable chair? Is the room quiet or do you hear other noises, birds singing, children playing, traffic going by? Are you glancing out of a window occasionally? Do you smell dinner cooking? Even as our primary focus is on one thing, such as reading, we are always bombarded by sensory stimuli, even when we are not paying attention.

The sense of sight is the one most used to navigate the world and the one that would be hardest to lose. Isn't it truly amazing the way the brain creates sight from light waves signaled by the eyes to the brain? The eyes are perfectly designed to take light waves that bounce off an object in through the pupil, cornea, then vitreous fluid focuses them on the bundle of optic nerves that send signals to the brain. And as unbelievable as it seems, the image goes to the brain upside down, but is corrected in the brain and we see the object right side up. Its shape, colors, and other distinguishing characteristics are in clear focus and we can make sense of our world.

The saying "the eyes are the windows of the soul" is a poetic way of expressing the wonder of seeing. When we look into someone's eyes we can see into their heart, and if we are astute, we can see their beauty and innocence. Another way of understanding this quote is to remember that the eyes are the windows through which the soul looks out into the world.

Another word for eyesight is vision. Both refer to physical seeing while vision can also mean an idea or mental image. Our most honored leaders have been known as visionaries who have inspired popular imagination of a better way that led to needed social change. A visionary looks at the world through the soul's eyes.

Through the eyes we can see beauty and love, but we can also see ugliness and despair. Through the eyes we can enter into another person's life and share their pain and heartache. We see with our eyes but also with our hearts and as visionaries we can see possibilities for a better world.

Taste is, perhaps, the sense we enjoy most, because we are aware of it at least three times a day. However, many times, we never stop to really enjoy our sense of taste; we live to eat, to feel full rather than enjoying the texture, the color and the tastes of food. We eat not because we are hungry, but because it is the time of day when we normally have our meals. If we skipped a meal we might lose weight and we certainly don't want to do that! We don't want to feel anything as unpleasant as hunger.

Food grown in the United States has lost the richness of the taste of food, straight from the garden or the orchard. To make up for the lack of taste, our food is filled with artificial flavorings, salt and sugar. Have you noticed how little real food is in our stores? Aisle after aisle contains nothing but processed items and junk food like chips and sodas. No wonder we are a nation of obese, unhealthy people.

When I traveled to Kenya, I was happily surprised at how good the food tasted because it was so fresh and not shipped across 3,000 miles. The food went straight from the backyard garden and orchard to the kitchen and the table. A growing trend to eat food grown within 100 miles of where we live is evidence of a new awareness about the relationship of food to health. For example, my son who lives in Jacksonville, Florida, is an avid gardener who grows many vegetables and makes organic baby food from his garden for his two grandchildren. The "fresh food" markets and farmers markets are bringing back the sense of taste even as the focus shifts to awareness of food as it is eaten and how it is grown and processed.

What we describe as flavor is usually a combination of taste, smell, temperature and texture. Our tongues have thousands of taste receptors called taste buds which send signals to the brain indicating whether food is sweet, salty, bitter or savory. Some recent research points to taste buds for calcium also. In fact, our perception of taste increases when more senses are engaged.

With our eyes we appreciate the beauty of a colorful plate of food, and with the sense of touch we experience the crunchy texture of raw fruits and vegetables and our mouth waters when we smell the odor of a wonderful meal.

Recently, a reception following a wedding featured a tiered table of nothing but chocolate treats. The chocolate dipped strawberries, chocolate covered nuts, chocolate cookies and candy created a chocolate lover's dream. Even the baskets holding the treats were made of chocolate. Every time I look at the picture on my iPhone my mouth starts watering. Such is the power of sight to engage the sense of taste.

Speaking of chocolate, my cousin has always been a chocoholic with an amazing sense of smell and for every birthday I bake a chocolate cake for her. On year I visited her in Atlanta to celebrate her birthday and hid her cake under the bed in the guest room. Still the minute she opened her apartment door she smelled the chocolate - *so much for the surprise.*

Animals have a much keener sense of smell than humans, but still we can recognize thousands of different smells. Our ability to smell is due to between 5 and 6 million cells located high up in the nasal passages. Taste and smell are closely linked and the main organ of taste as well as smell is the human nose.

Since our tongues can only distinguish four distinct tastes, sweet, salty, bitter and sour all other tastes are a result of the stimulation of the olfactory nerves. Next time you eat, notice how the sense of taste is strong on the back of the tongue and as we breathe the smell of the food is enhanced and our enjoyment increased. (The Smell Report-Social Issues Research Center) Beginning as early as age thirty, our sense of smell begins to fade, and is not as sharp as it once was.

Through awareness and exercises, however, we can maintain and even increase our sense of smell. For example, workers at the Philadelphia Water Department are trained to detect subtle odors that denote problems and thus ensure the water's quality.

Something as simple as taking time to smell our food and our coffee before tasting it, smelling spices, perfumes or flowers will exercise this olfactory function and enable our sense of smell. A keen sense of smell affords us more enjoyment of our food and our lives. Research published in the Wall Street Journal - Ellen Byron, February, 2013.

A new science is being developed called smell-centered communication and soon smells will be sent over the iPhone. If friends are having a meal in a wonderful Mediterranean restaurant, they will be able to send the aroma of the food to us to make us jealous. Imagine receiving the smell of the North woods and a mountain stream on a steamy hot August day. Marketers are already piping in smells that make us want to buy their products.

Smells are the portals of happy and unhappy memories. A special family holiday with our favorite holiday foods, allows us to re-run the scene later and recall happy times. Depending on one's ethnic heritage, the smell of curry or of a charcoal fire with hamburgers cooking brings back memories of home. One of the casualties of modern life is the lack of smells of food cooking in the family kitchen. How sad for children who have never come home from school to the smell of cookies baking.

The smell of a stable or of a horse can elicit memories of childhood long gone and flood the memory bank with a news-reel of images. The smell of Evening in Paris perfume stirs memories of Mothers and Grandmothers and long ago. For me, the smell of the cypress walls in Cotton Hall, the Swamp Gravy theatre, brings back memories or many years of performances.

A "rural legend" in our town is that my Cousin's husband was going on a fishing trip with his buddies. My Cousin was not happy with his choice of friends for this trip, so when she packed his suitcase she generously sprayed his clothes with her perfume. When he arrived at his destination and started to unpack, he smelled her perfume and decided fishing was not his priority and returned home. Such is the power of perfume, memory and emotions.

Our sense of hearing is also one of Nature's gifts for our enjoyment. The heartfelt word of love, as well as words of encouragement and inspiration fill our hearts and lift our spirits. The sounds of music, the rhapsody of birds, waterfalls, mountain streams, rain on the roof, even the clap of thunder tunes us in to beauty that is all around us.

Hearing begins before birth and remains until the time of death, even if people are in a coma. Babies respond to their Mother's voices in utero and even recognize it after birth, as reported by Meghan Holohan on NBC news in August 2013. Babies react to sounds in the womb such as certain music and respond to the same melody when they are born. We are told that hearing is the last sense to leave just before death. Doctors encourage family members to talk to patients even though they appear unresponsive, and to play music that will bring them comfort.

The auditory system is extremely sensitive and can be easily damaged and because we are bombarded by jarring noises, our hearing is probably our most abused sense. Even if we try to avoid boom boxes, and night clubs and keep the volume down on our TVs, we are still the victims of loud screeching and screaming noises such as sirens, traffic noises, lawn mowers and weed eaters. My pet peeve is the unnecessary loudness of movies and the advertisements before the movie begins. They are maddening!

I carry earplugs and try to enjoy the movie even while I am going deaf.

Music is a source of pleasure for us and we associate certain songs with certain periods of our lives. Songs bring back memories of romance, or periods of history. My brother was a Marine in the jungles of Vietnam. When I think of that sad time, the song "Johnny, Don't Be a Hero" comes to my mind. And who could ever forget the Beatles and the songs of that era, especially, "Imagine All the People"? I am very fond of the song "Wind Beneath My Wings" because it reminds me of the people who have encouraged me and lifted me up throughout my life.

As people begin to lose their hearing they can be teasingly accused of selective hearing; that is hearing what they want to hear and tuning out everything else. Likewise, we tune out political views that don't agree with ours and facts that don't correspond with our world view. We are comfortable in our mental laziness and don't want to be challenged to think in a new way. We also tune out things that cause us pain that we feel we cannot impact. We don't want to hear the crying of the hurting world.

Many people are not comfortable with silence and have the TV or radio turned on even if they are not consciously listening. If we train ourselves to listen to beautiful sounds we can meditate into the deep silence which is the sound of the Universe.

The skin is the largest sense organ and protects our body from bacteria, dehydration, physical and chemical toxins. Our skin regulates body temperature, produces vitamin D and repairs itself after injury. We take for granted its multiple functions in keeping us comfortable and enhancing our lives. Through our skin we sense temperature, (hot and cold), textures (rough and smooth), pressure (tight and loose), discomfort (burning and itching) and many other sensations. Through our skin we know the pleasure of closeness to another person whether in the act of shaking hands, a passionate embrace or hugging a child.

Hugging is a form of communication that gives an emotional lift to both parties. Virginia Satir, a noted family therapist, is credited with commenting that we need four hugs a day for survival, eight for maintenance and twelve for growth. The most benefit can be gained if the hug lasts 20 seconds and is a full heart to heart hug. Hugs release oxytocin, a hormone which stimulates a mood of happiness and has been called the bliss hormone. Hugs also release serotonin which negates feelings of loneliness, anger and isolation. National Hug Day is celebrated on January 21 and is observed in many cities. People walking in city squares are taken by surprise by a number of 'free hug' signs and hugs shared by strangers, which lends an air of exuberance and joy to an otherwise staid, mind your own business environment.

Of course, in most our experiences, we take in information from all five senses at once-as in my description of the Florida beach at the beginning of this chapter. Also, it has been noted that some people can cross-sense, for instance, they can taste colors or music, or hear the cries of plants that are being abused. Most of us, however, favor one sense over the others.

Many years ago some friends and I organized a gourmet food manufacturing company and sold our products at wholesale gift shows all over the US. It was an education in the use of the senses to watch people as they approached our booth. The interior designers would exclaim over the beautiful green and white display, with miniature lights illuminating glass brick. They enjoyed life and appreciated beauty through the sense of sight.

Those, whose sense of smell was their keenest sense, could smell the Vidalia onions we used in our salad dressings and would comment about the delicious smells even before they stopped to taste the products. Closely related, were the tasters, and since we had wonderful samples of our products for tasting, they really enjoyed themselves, especially the jelly made from port wine. Invariably, they were the good cooks and sometimes their figures showed their love of food.

Those whose hearing was their strongest sense would listen intently to our sales pitch and ask questions while weighing their decisions. The women who were touchers would run their hands over the embroidered lace tablecloth and the glass brick and would feel the texture of the baskets and the coolness of the canning jars. These women were always beautifully dressed in rich, sensuous fabrics. Recognizing the strongest sense tells a lot about personalities and life choices.

Researchers point to many more senses than the primary five, at least twenty more. Many of these are in the category of intuition or a gut feeling such as the feeling that someone is looking at us or that someone is in the room before the physical senses acknowledge their presence.

Sometimes a strange sensation in the body warns when the barometer drops just before a storm or of a sudden temperature change. Many other senses are familiar but often unacknowledged such as emotional feelings of being loved, nurtured, and cared for, or an intuitive sense of danger for a loved one. Sensations of anticipation, and excitement, a sense of right and wrong, a sense of happiness or joy, a sense of gratitude or thankfulness are among the many ways we experience physical reality.

While many people are alienated from senses and their sensual nature, super-sensitive people have a heightened awareness of sensory stimuli and experience sounds louder, colors more vivid, emotions felt more keenly. Icons of sensuality like Mae West, Marilyn Monroe or Madonna, are sometimes viewed with suspicion and jealousy because they glory in their sensuality.

Our bodies are wonderfully complex systems but we abuse them in multiple ways: through stress, over-eating, and yo-yo dieting, for example. We live in our intellect, our minds and seldom pay attention to our bodies, except when we get a signal that something is amiss: we are tired or thirsty or in pain. Our bodies are used to serve what we believe to be a higher goal like making a living and we forget to enjoy every experience for its own sake.

A friend in Jaffrey, N.H. invited me for lunch at her new condo located on a rushing mountain stream. When we arrived, she led us to the kitchen counter where a mound of white peony blossoms were lying, stripped from their stems. We were invited to sink our hands and arms into the mound of blossoms and rub them over our faces and necks. This was one of the most amazing and unforgettable sensual experiences of my life. As we pay attention to our senses and our sensuality, we can grow joyfully in our enjoyment of life.

What if we spent a day simply enjoying our senses through the beauty of nature and to look for sensual experiences to make the body come alive? We could also make a ritual of tasting our food and drink and celebrating the closeness to special people by sharing physical contact such as hugging.

It is important to develop the outer senses which are paramount through our bodies, but it is equally important to develop the internal intuitive senses and feelings, so I invite you to explore other levels of sensing in the following ways: pay attention to the small details, to subtle intuitions, to relationships, to feelings about retirement.

Many occasions present themselves to pay attention to the little things in life, for instance: note where you put keys, glasses, cup of coffee, and the mail. How much time would we gain if weren't constantly looking for something. I stopped by a friend's house to give her a gift and when I started to leave I could not find my car keys. A young policeman graciously came over and unlocked my car (the beauty of living in a small town) but my keys were not in my car. I was about to panic, and I dreaded calling my husband. All of a sudden my friend's husband pulled them out of his pocket; he had picked them up thinking they were his. So pay attention to whose keys you pocket.

We are so distracted by the demands and interests of our lives that we do not pay attention to the subtle feelings that are constantly with us. A sense of mindfulness about the myriad feelings that run through our bodies is a way of accessing unconscious material in our psyches. When we are around some people we may feel relaxed and at peace and harmony. Around others we may feel excitement and anticipation of the way the interaction will progress.

Other, not so pleasant feelings, such as dread, unease or distrust, signal that something needs our attention. We want to run away from the person but if we stop and pay attention, the encounter can become an avenue for personal growth. Many times these signals are felt physically, such as indigestion or a stomach ache, tightness in the chest, or flushing of the skin. Popular culture has descriptions for these states, such as "He is a pain in the butt", or "He makes me want to cuss a cat", or "She gives me the heebie-jeebies."

When a person rubs us like sandpaper, we can learn from these emotions that rise up in us. Emotions of anger, irritation, are signals to look deeply at the part of ourselves that is being reflected back to us and shows us our shadow side. It may be that what is being reflected back to us in a mirror of our own judgment or envy or mean spiritedness.

Sometimes we meet someone for the first time and immediately dislike them only to discover that the attributes that we disliked are our own worst personality traits. We are turned off by their loud laughter and attention seeking because we want to be the center of attention. We may be turned off by someone's "pity party" because our compassion has hit a dry spell.

Our internal reactions to others can be one of our greatest teachers. As you pay attention to healthy and unhealthy relationships, you can be mindful of those you love to be around, as well as those who need you, and those who only use you. Some acquaintances build you up and some tear you down and you can consciously choose how you will relate to them. You can become aware of those people who push your buttons and why. What is the real basis of the reaction that is raising its ugly head when certain people appear? Perhaps your primary way of relating is as the victim or the judge. Is it possible that your conversation is mostly in the "ain't it awful" way of relating?

If you are nearing retirement you may want to pay attention to your feelings about retirement. For some people, retirement can bring not only decline in income, but loss of purpose, loss of a reason to get up every day, and loss of work-friendship circle. This is one of the biggest changes that a person faces in his lifetime. I have known several people who retired after building an organization to a level of high performance under their command. They were surprised and hurt that the ensuing leadership never acknowledged their contribution, asked for advice or kept them in the loop in any way. 'Gone and forgotten' seems to be the modus operandi. Many people experience depression after retirement due to these feelings of not being appreciated.

The history of the achievements of the company, or not-for-profit, where they worked and gave so much of their life and vital energy goes unrecognized and unappreciated. It is as though the present fell straight out of heaven and had not been built consciously and with skill and dedication. Just to acknowledge these feelings is helpful as a way of letting go and moving on. Be aware that it is not personal but is the norm in business and non-profit venues.

As you approach retirement you may want to pay attention to where you can donate your time and talent to make a difference in the world. You may be led to follow your heart and expand your world by stepping outside of your comfort zone. If you volunteer at a soup kitchen or other social services agency, getting to know the people you are serving will rescue you from the "blame the victim" mind- set.

Sitting in judgment on people who are in unfortunate circumstances is easy unless we know their situation and have walked in their shoes. Just by giving our full attention and listening to a person's story you acknowledge their experiences and give meaning to their lives. As you pay attention to the larger life you are called to live, beyond your little materialistic, egoic concerns, you can acknowledge the past and move into the future with new experiences, new friends and new reasons to live.

You can pay attention to the nudges of Spirit calling to move into the world of service. As we pay attention to our senses, and to the internal nudges we will feel more alive. I invite you to read on.

Go Deeper

In my tool box of gardening tools I have chosen the lavender plant as a metaphor for paying attention. The lavender plant has blossoms which range in color from lavender to indigo blue and fields of lavender are very beautiful. It is plant that calls forth the use of all senses. Our eyes are enchanted by the graceful spikes of color, the wonderful smell perfumes sachets and is a repellent for moths. Our taste buds respond to the flavor in candy and other treats. And its essential oil helps heal our body and soothe our spirit.

○ When and where has the beauty of the world made you feel like you are standing on tip toe in wonder and amazement? Take a visit back to that time and place in your creative imagination.

○ What is your favorite fragrance? Is it the smell of certain flowers or an expensive perfume?

○ When have you gotten in trouble because you were not paying attention?

○ Do you sometimes smell trouble?

Go Lightly

○ Buy a lavender plant and experiment with its different gifts to the senses.

○ Plan a Sabbath as a day to enjoy your senses through the beauty of Nature. Try counting the different bird calls that you hear or the number of different shades of green that you see.

○ Look for sensual experiences to make your body come alive, maybe sleep on satin sheets or walk in the rain or have a massage.

Renascence

(Excerpt)

"The world stands out on either side
No wider than the heart is wide;
Above the world is stretched the sky,
No higher than the soul is high.
The heart can push the sea and land
Farther away on either hand;
The soul can split the sky in two,
And let the face of God shine through.
But East and West will pinch the heart
That cannot keep them pushed apart;
And he whose soul is flat ---- the sky
Will cave in on him by and by."

Edna St. Vincent Millay

Aurora Leigh

"*Earth's crammed with heaven*
And every common bush afire with God.
But he who sees takes off his shoes
The rest sit round and pluck blackberries."

Elizabeth Barrett Browning

CHAPTER THREE

ACT ALIVE

"Just being alive is a call for rapture." Rumi

In this poem, Elizabeth Barrett Browning paints a word picture of being alive. In a mystical description of beauty, Earth's crammed with heaven, she speaks of her response to this amazing beauty. Using Biblical imagery from the Old Testament of Moses' encounter with God, at the burning bush, she contrasts aliveness with lack of awareness. Those who are unaware are tending to the business at hand, not having the ultimate experience the moment affords. They are half asleep to the wonders of life and have little appreciation of the moment, much less that they should take off their shoes in awe.

Howard Thurman has been credited with saying, "What the world needs is people who have come alive.

Don't ask what the world needs; ask what makes you come alive." Nothing fills me with the rapture of being alive like being in Nature. My favorite place is the boardwalk across the wetlands at Spring Creek Park in my hometown. On this beautiful April day the multitudes of different shades of green are contrasted against a vibrant blue sky. The honeysuckle vine is running in long swaths of intoxicating perfume. The Cherokee rose's virginal white blossoms dance in the soft breezes.

What a feast for the senses. The water is a perfect mirror and to gaze into these depths is to explore another dimension of time. Watching reflections in the water is an opportunity to enter into the spiritual depths of one's soul. Such beauty allows time for stillness and introspection.

We interact each day with family, friends and acquaintances that are constantly complaining and have become angry and bitter as they face the problems of life. They live out of feelings of depression, grieving, envy, jealousy and are emotionally and physically draining on those near them. Others can be referred to as the 'walking dead' because they are stuck in routine and old patterns of thinking and acting and refuse to consider any other ways.

In contrast, aliveness is living above and beyond and in spite of present circumstances. To be alive, is to live in the moment, not shut down by habit, or expectation, but always in an attitude of expectancy.

Zorba explains, "They say that age kills the fire inside of a man and when he hears death coming, he opens the door and says, 'Come in, give me rest.' That is a bunch of lies. I've got enough fire in me to devour the world, so I fight." Nikos Kazantzakis' "Zorba the Greek."

Rumi reminds us that "Just being alive is a call for rapture." My most vivid memory of falling into rapture was when I visited the UNESCO Heritage site, magnificent Iguazu Falls, located on the border of Brazil, Argentina and Paraguay. Being in the presence of such grandeur surrounded by hundreds of rainbows transported me into a state of ecstasy, and was an unrepeatable moment of Grace.

Nature has been called a magic well that the more we drink from the more we are replenished. The more we know about nature, the more complete our enjoyment can become as our knowledge informs our senses and deepens our appreciation. To personally know trees, or roses or breeds of dogs, is to enjoy them more deeply. This knowing allows the enlargement of the senses, the imagination, and the intelligence and grows new pathways in the brain.

When we are fully alive we are open to surprise. These, A-Ha moments, announce themselves when the light bulb goes off in our consciousness. The sudden flash of insight is a signal that we are living in the now but we are also making connections that give new meaning to our experiences. Great literature and meaningful conversation can be instruments which provide such moments as we share from the depths of our being. Poetry is one of my favorite ways to find these moments of delight. For instance, the poem that Edna St. Vincent Millay wrote as a college student has been a source of inspiration for me for many years. This excerpt reads:

> *"The world stands out on either side*
> *No wider than the heart is wide;*
> *Above the world is stretched the sky,*
> *No higher than the soul is high.*
> *The heart can push the sea and land*
> *Farther away on either hand;*
> *The soul can split the sky in two,*

And let the face of God shine through.
But East and West will pinch the heart
That cannot keep them pushed apart;
And he whose soul is flat–the sky
Will cave in on him by and by.

What does it mean to be alive? Is it to feel deeply? When we feel deeply we also are aware of the burdens, sadness and sorrow that are part of life and the agony of being human. We grieve with friends in their losses of spouses and children. We endure our own physical pain with stoicism. Our physical and emotional pain can drive us inward and we begin to live in a cocoon of our own suffering. We can shut down because we don't want to feel pain, and we can turn a blind eye to suffering of others. We can become depressed, disillusioned and even despairing. When we begin to live in this place of psychic pain, we can seek relief by creating 'drama' and chaos around us. And we seek sympathy by constantly recounting our symptoms to all who will listen. On the other hand, we can turn any time of grief or despair into a time of encouragement for others by our courageous attitude.

Laughter is certainly a part of feeling alive. As we laugh we relax and let go of tension and built up emotion that can be toxic.

To be alive is to be curious. Quincy Jones, the famous musician, reminds us always to be nosy, that will energize us. An alive person is always searching for new experiences because the brain longs for stimulation. When we are alive we are open to the new, to wonder. It's almost like falling in love, maybe it is falling in love, in love with life and possibility.

Through movies we experience the emotional and physical life of others, through exercise and physical activity we explore bodily reactions, and through availing ourselves of opportunities to study with great minds we expand our intellectual abilities. The task is to reach out and search for ways to be involved in the on-going drama of what it means to be human.

The recent movie, *The Best Exotic Marigold Hotel*, illustrates different adaptations to like's changes. The story describes the lives of seven people from England, who in their retirement years, find that unforeseen circumstances have caused them to move to India to seek an affordable lifestyle. Some of the characters face change with courage and an adventurous spirit in spite of the culture shock, the heat, the noise and the press of people. Others are stuck in the illusions of their youth, that sex and money are the answer. Others seek and find redemption and closure to wounds of the past and are able to find a new life. The movie is an amazing study of human adaptability in the latter years. In each of the stories we can see ourselves and our various approaches to change.

Eleanor Roosevelt reminds us to do one thing every day that scares us. Taking healthy creative risks makes us feel very alive. I feel most alive when I am on a stage speaking to an audience because this act engages my intellect, my self-confidence, my ability to relate to an audience, my charm and charisma. I am operating on all burners.

When and where do you feel most alive?

News correspondents who choose to go into the war zones, called hot spots, to get the latest story were asked why they chose to live this way. They live in constant danger and leave their families and homes for months at the time. Their answers were related to the fact that the excitement, danger, and constant challenge makes them feel alive. People who become addicted to the rush of adrenaline in demanding situations, we call these people dare devils, and we marvel at their exploits as they race down the ski slopes or the Indianapolis Speedway. They test the limits of their skill and endurance and are cited as our heroes. We are transfixed by the Olympics, America's Ninja Warriors, and by the skill and discipline these athletes exhibit.

Our lives are on a continuum between agony and ecstasy, and we are happiest when we live with these extremes perfectly balanced, not tipping the scales too much in either direction. We don't want to experience suffering or invite the hubris of too much happiness. So we settle down and shut down and settle for lives of quiet desperation. We are willing to live vicariously through the latest sports hero or "reality" TV personality.

David Whyte's poem reminds us that we are constantly in a state of change and fluidity:

"We shape ourselves to fit the world
And by the world are shaped again.
The visible and invisible together
In common cause to produce the miraculous."

This poem reminds us that we are constantly changed by the pressures and expectations of the world. We impact everything in our world and consequently are impacted by everything. The visible is the outward circumstances and invisible can be seen as angels, the Hand of God, or the Field of all possibilities. No matter the name we give this, we are the benefactors of the miraculous every day.

Yes, there are days when we are so alive that we feel reborn. Is this what Jesus meant when he said "You must be born again," as we see everything with fresh eyes, with wonder and amazement? To feel in the depth of your being, the unmatched glory of life. Is this what it means to 'wake up' as the Buddha expresses it?

As I write, I am aware that to practice aliveness is very difficult. Is it when we are in the face of death that we are most truly alive? In day-to-day living, our goal may be to be fully present in the moment, to really notice what is happening around us, to us and within us. If we can encounter every experience in joy and appreciation and live with heart open, senses alert and at one with the Presence in unity of body, mind and Spirit, then we are truly alive. The Kingdom of Heaven is here and now in experiences such as this.

Rituals, ceremonies and celebrations can also bring us a sense of aliveness and give continuity, meaning and richness to daily life. These are the reminders that there is more to life than living on the "surface crust of consciousness" as Jean Houston aptly states.

Family rituals, like reading a bedtime story; celebrating the extended family at family reunions; weddings, holidays, baptisms, and remembering those in need on holidays are important parts of family life. Rituals rehearse the values and the stories that bind us as families and communities. They take us to another place in our memory, imagination and experience and can be seen as part of the cultural DNA. As we enumerate our values, we can create and share rituals which celebrate these values. We can enjoy the rituals and celebrations of other cultures and create bonds of understanding and friendship.

At the end of each Swamp Gravy performance, the ritual of lighting candles, calling the names of those whose memory we cherish, while singing Amazing Grace, takes us into the depth of remembering. Even though we may not have known any of the people whose names are called, we are brought to a place of reverence and sanctity.

One can go to any religious heritage to find the rituals that comfort and nourish. In the Tibetan Buddhist tradition, the practice of "ton glen" helps us to transmute suffering into blessings for all the earth. The saints and mystics teach us to live in the presence of Soul, in the quiet place where all is well. When we are truly alive we radiate our light, our vibration is high and we attract others to share our journey as we lift the vibration of the world.

As we seek to live dynamically, may our radiance and aliveness be a beacon that lights the way to a more sustainable world.

Go Deeper

The color that I have in my box of paints that symbolizes aliveness is the *color orange*. And since I am a redhead I like to think about living as though my "hair is on fire." Zorba reminds us that he has enough fire inside to devour the world. Fire is a great transformer giving light to the night. As it burns it purifies, gives warmth, heat for cooking, and fuel to run our machinery. We are mesmerized as flames of fire do a beautiful dance of aliveness.

o   What activities make you feel most alive?

o   Is it physical exercise and exertion?

o   Is it reading beautiful poetry or listening to a symphony?

o   Journal about a time when you fell into rapture.

Go Lightly

o Build a fire in a fire pit and watch the flames.

o Dance to any music that calls to you, the CD "Hooked on Classics" is my favorite.

o Write a Haiku about being alive. Here is mine.

I stumped my toe
The pain reminded me that
I am still alive.

◦ Watch an animal use all of his senses as he peruses his world.

Happiness to Be Had

There is happiness to be had
It hovers in the air waiting
for you to embrace it

Let it come in and attach little wings to your heart
so you all can hang out with hope
in the light places

These are challenging days for empaths
turn off the news
be your own best story.

Leah Mann

CHAPTER FOUR

ACCEPT CHALLENGE

"Bite Off More Than You Can Chew, **Then** *Chew It."*
Maggie Kuhn, Founder of the Gray Panthers.

Around 1964, I read Betty Friedan's book, "The Feminine Mystique," which changed the life of so many women of my generation. My own psyche was profoundly impacted, and I started dreaming that I was on a college campus, experiencing great happiness. In 1967, my third child, my daughter, was born and I told my husband about my recurrent dream. His answer greatly surprised me when he said, "I think you should go back to college."

I had dropped out of undergraduate studies after two years to get married. So I started back to finish my undergraduate degree when I was 34 years old; my boys were 4 and 10 and my baby 8 months old. I had to drive 60 miles each way to attend class on a large university campus, which was unheard of in my small South Georgia town in the late 1960's. The first morning as I was on the way to register for classes, I had car trouble 15 miles from home. I was scared and almost lost my confidence as I kept wondering, if this was a sign that I should turn back and forget the whole thing. I was going with my husband's blessing, but against the wishes of my in-laws and my parents.

Each semester there was a challenge of finding the right child care in Tallahassee, FL. Three meals a day had to be prepared, the household continued, but I had to study. My biggest challenge was the semester that my husband and one child went to bed with the mumps, and I had to write 11 papers. I promise you that my husband did not raise his head off the pillow even to eat. My professors were very understanding and I finally graduated with a Master's Degree in Social Work in 1976, 12 years after reading Betty Friedan's seminal work.

Meeting these challenges prepared me to accept many more and led to my life unfolding into one that Jean Houston calls "a mythic life." My career as a professional social worker took me into many demanding situations, such as homes without running water or sanitary facilities. I learned not to be afraid, but to forge ahead, even to the point of going through the Court system to take children out of these homes and put them into foster care.

This courage served me well, and I became a community organizer with an innate understanding of how to bring interested people together to design approaches to address a common problem. I was considered a trouble-maker by some because I crossed the racial divide in my small Southern town when I accompanied an African American woman to the polls to vote.

Later, I organized an entrepreneurial business to create employment in my poverty ridden area. Then I became an Arts advocate at the State level. Now I am a social activist on many platforms including issues like affordable housing, local foods, prison reform, as well as using the arts for community development.

Facing these challenges changed my life and thus the lives of others. What about you? What are the challenges that you have faced and that have prepared you for your life today? Accepting challenges whether we are completely successful or not (I have lots of unfinished projects) helps to build confidences and self-esteem. It opens doors to new friends and new experiences and causes us to grow in ways we could not have imagined. As Jean Houston says, "We do not bore God."

It doesn't seem fair, but as we get older, the more demanding life becomes. We love our comfortable life style, even with its obligations and our aches and pains. We don't want to get out of our routine, and sometimes prefer boredom to challenge. But life has a way of throwing us into new situations, and we have to find new ways of coping.

When Hugh Downs left the "Today Show," he suggested that we should "re-pot" ourselves every 10 years. Hugh Downs was talking about making a career change that offered new opportunities, skills, and friends. We may not want to re-pot ourselves, but we can re-invigorate ourselves by accepting the challenges that come into our lives. After all, challenge makes us feel alive.

The several different kinds of challenges can be classified as physical, mental, emotional or spiritual or maybe they are a combination of all of the above. We face physical challenges when we fall and have a broken bone or have a debilitating illness. A mental challenge may come in the form of dealing with the IRS to pay our taxes or learning a new computer program, an emotional challenge may be a result of a divorce or death in the family, and a spiritual challenge may be a crisis in faith caused by a hardship in any of these areas.

I have chosen to classify challenges in a different way. For instance, one type of challenge is one that you choose and/or create for yourself, like the things on your "to-do" bucket list? I always thought I wanted to ride a mule down into the Grand Canyon. That is, until I saw the Grand Canyon and reality set in. Maybe some of the things still on your bucket list could be done in a modified form. Every pretty day an acquaintance takes his para-glider for a low hanging fly over our town. Maybe that equates with a ride down the Grand Canyon. The challenge for me would be to trust myself to lift off in something that looks like a rainbow with a motor. Or I may settle for a ride on a roller coaster or a Ferris wheel.

On a more serious note, becoming involved in the local foods movement is my friend Juby Phillips' way of checking an item off her bucket list. She led her church in planting a raised-bed vegetable garden and sharing the produce with her local soup kitchen through a program called "Food For A Thousand," and is now planting community gardens in many parks and public spaces.

Another friend, Jan Selman, an artist and an activist is dedicated to encouraging women to serve in the political arena. She has become disgusted by the polarization in our government and believes that women are much more likely to "cross the aisle" and work for the common good. Jan, a feisty redhead, travels the state of Georgia interviewing women who are already in office, hearing their stories and learning from them. She also meets women who have political aspirations and encourages them through the arduous election process. This kind of behind the scenes activism, which includes mentoring and cheerleading, creates new possibilities for collaboration and real change.

Another kind of challenge is the one we can reject. When someone asks us to do something, and we have a gut feeling that we should not, then we must listen to our bodies. It is O.K. to say "No", without guilt, to requests and demands. We can begin to feel overworked and under-loved if we allow encroachment on our person. We can refuse to be caught up in other people's agendas. Real strength is required to set limits and not be used beyond our comfort level. But be careful that we are not saying "no" out of selfishness or pride.

Probably, we are most conflicted by challenges that are thrust upon us by family, friends or life circumstances. These are the hard ones and while we would not choose them, we cannot say no to them. The challenge of a disabled child puts strain on a marriage, that the marriage many times cannot survive. All of the emotional energy goes to care for the child and no energy is left for the relationship. Not only the stress, but add the anger, guilt or depression, and life is almost overwhelming.

The many women and men who are raising grandchildren and even great-grandchildren are the real heroes of our day. Talk about being tired and stressed at the end of the day. Another new trend in family life brought about by the downturn in the economy is that young adults are moving back home to live with their parents. This shift in roles between parent and child to parent and grown child is a difficult transition. The challenge of dealing across generations in families is a poignant, universal story.

One of the most poignant stories in the Swamp Gravy play "The Gospel Truth," is a story told by a woman who was abandoned by her mother and raised by her Grandmother. She never expected to see her Mother again, but when her Mother got very sick and needed her, she took her in and cared for her, in a most tender way, until she died. This story was told to illustrate the Ten Commandment that instructs us to "Honor Thy Father and Thy Mother." The scene ends with the lines, "she didn't raise me, but that's something she has to settle with the Lord, not me. I did what the Lord told me to do." The challenge of dealing across generations in families is a universal story.

My story is not so dramatic nor far-reaching, but it was pivotal in my understanding, of how to meet a challenge, that comes out of the blue as a request from family. I had relatives living in Brazil whose son was working on an oil rig, in the Gulf of Mexico, off the coast of New Orleans. His parents had not heard from him for months, and all efforts to reach him had failed. Although he had been a Navy Seal and could take care of himself, his family was worried about him. I was flabbergasted when they called me from Brazil one day and asked me to help them find their son.

New Orleans is seven hours by car, and I could not understand why or how they thought I might be able to find him. I was dumb founded. How was I, sitting in a little town in South Georgia, going to find a young man missing somewhere between New Orleans and the Gulf of Mexico? Then I remembered the adage that there are only five degrees of separation between any two people in the world. At that point I was in my entrepreneur phase and remembered the man who was the sales representative in Louisiana for our line of jellies and salad dressings. I called him, with no information except a name. In three hours he called me back and he had found the missing son. My contact was a former Catholic priest who "worked the streets" for the Red Cross and knew how to use the networks, just like in the movies. He considered it all in a day's work; I considered it a miracle.

Sometimes the unexpected tragedies of life call forth heroic action that causes nationwide impact. We know many stories of living people who have turned the greatest tragedy of their lives into a victory for change and justice.   Donna Norris turned her daughter's kidnapping and murder into the Amber Alert, which has created concern for missing children in the whole country.

Agnes Furey, my most recent heroine, was almost crushed by the murder of her daughter and six year old grandson by an addicted man who her daughter was trying to rehabilitate. Seven years after the murder, in an attempt to understand, Agnes reached out to Leonartd Scoven who is serving a life sentence without parole. Agnes and Leonard began a correspondence that has been turned into a book called "Wildflowers in the Median" and a play by the same name. Agnes has become a powerful force in the restorative justice movement in Florida as well as nationally.

Mythic heroes have faced unbelievable hardships and have risen to the task placed upon them. We immediately think of Lincoln, Gandhi, Martin Luther King, Jr., Mother Teresa, Jackie Robinson, Nelson Mandela and other lesser known contemporary people like Vandana Shiva, who constantly challenges multi-national corporations for their destruction of India's national resources for corporate profit. Maybe you would like to tell a story to a grandchild or close friend about an ordinary person that accepted an extraordinary challenge and their impact on you.

Larger than life people inspire us with their courage and dedication to a cause. One of my favorite heroes is Joe Bowen of Kentucky, who rode a bicycle across the United States twice. Not only that, but in 1980, he walked on stilts 3,000 miles across the U.S. to raise money for Muscular Dystrophy. He was awarded the Kentucky Unbridled Spirit Award by his home state, a well-deserved honor.

My home is only 90 miles from Jimmy Carter's hometown, Plains, GA. President Carter is a mythic hero to me because he has used the power of his status as former President to impact issues of critical importance, such as health, housing for the poor and peace. He was awarded the Nobel Peace Prize in 2002 for his untiring efforts for peace and human rights. Recently, it was announced that his initiative has eradicated the guinea worm in Africa, thus saving countless people from terrible suffering. Even though he is in his nineties now and Rosalyn is in her late eighties, they have not slowed down their efforts to bring their resources of prestige and contacts to work for peace and justice all over the world.

Another of my mythic heroes is Dietrich Bonhoeffer, the young German theologian who chose to defy the Nazis. He was sent to a concentration camp and hanged just days before the liberation. His poem

"Who Am I?" shows the internal struggle of his Spirit in those dark days as he grappled with the external perception that his captors saw, a man of kindness and courage and the internal feelings of loneliness and defeat. His resolution of the questions that tormented him is in the last lines of the poem:

Am I really all that which other men tell of
Or Am I only what I myself know of myself?
Who Am I?
They mock me, these lonely questions of mine.
Whoever I am, Thou knowest, O God, I am Thine.

The most difficult kinds of challenges are the ones that we know we have to accept or we cannot live. We cannot close our hearts to these opportunities or something within us will die. We do not choose them; they choose us, since we've been prepared by our training, interest and temperament to step up into this moment in history. These are calls from our soul.

I was working in the public welfare system in the 1980s and saw the dire need for day care for children of the working poor. The day I realized I could not die happy unless I had tried to meet this challenge, I called a local African-American woman who was a retired teacher. We started meeting with six other women who formed a non-profit board. We struggled to get 501-C-3 status for three years because not-for-profit day care was a new and radical idea. In the meantime, we had to figure out how to make the cost affordable to the families but also charge enough to pay the teacher, the rent and the food costs. We were successful, and this organization lasted 20 years, providing early learning, stimulation, food and safety to hundreds of children. It closed when our society finally recognized the importance of Head Start, pre-K, and kindergarten for all children.

Maggie Kuhn, founder of the Gray Panthers,

challenged herself to do something outrageous once a week. On Maggie Kuhn's birthday people remember her by doing something outrageous in her honor. What can you do that would be outrageous on Aug. 3? My friend, who is a fundraiser extraordinaire, tried to get us to pose for a nude calendar. Now that would be outrageous. We were game but thought better of it when we realized no-one would buy pictures of partially covered 80-year-old women, not even our husbands.

Challenges that we accept can make a profound difference in our lives. During my career as a social worker I witnessed the tragedy caused by addiction and have had a long held desire to organize a recovery group. The challenge and opportunity came through my local church to interact with incarcerated men on Sunday evenings. As I lead a 12 Step program I share their struggles, their guilt and pain caused by their addiction, and become part of the suffering of their world. The great divide between an older, white, well-to-do woman and these men of different ages and races has been crossed as we share from our hearts and our experiences. In many ways, these men are my best friends because we connect on a deep level.

As we stay informed, the issues of the world can be depressing because we see so much needless suffering. We can lose not only heart but faith in the ultimate triumph of good over evil. Our faith can be questioned even to the crisis point called "the dark night of the soul" that we all experience and mystics and saints write about. The inner disciplines of meditation and prayer is always available to give us strength. In the process we may discover new writers, poets and rituals that bring us the comfort and hope that sustains us.

As we decide to become more involved we can follow the path of the mystic, the servant, the seeker, the poet or the social activists. Whatever challenge life thrusts upon us we will find our hearts expanded, our friendships deepened, our intellect grown and our lives much more dynamic.

Go Deeper

The symbol I have chosen for this chapter is wine, deep and dark and rich. Wine, the drink, is a source of stimulation as well as relaxation. Wine, the beverage, represents transformation through fermentation. The grapes are crushed, even as challenges and difficulties of life can crush us and turn us into wine.

○ What are the challenges that you have faced that have made you the person you are today?

○ What is your greatest challenge at present?

o What is the best way you are rising to this challenge?

o Is there a ritual, a prayer, a meditation that helps you cope with this challenge?

Through the process of rising to challenges we become different people and are full of power to bless and share with others.

o How are you being turned into fine wine?

Go Lightly

o To be inspired by someone who has conquered many challenges, watch Aimee Mullins on TedTalks.

o Go to a wine festival and stomp grapes.

o Give a party to 'wine and dine' with friends.

o Toast yourself for your accomplishments as you rise to challenges.

Prospective Immigrants Please Note

Either you will
go through this door
or you will not go through.

If you go through
there is always the risk
of remembering your name.

Things look at you doubly
and you must look back
and let them happen.

If you do not go through
it is possible
to live worthily

to maintain your attitudes
to hold your position
to die bravely

but much will blind you,
much will evade you,
at what cost who knows?

The door itself
makes no promises.
It is only a door.

Adrienne Rich

CHAPTER FIVE

FIND ADVENTURE

"I Came into the World to LIVE Out Loud"
Emile Zola

My sister and I grew up on the family farm about a mile from our country town. We had electricity, but no telephone, much less a TV and no close neighbors. When we would complain of being bored, our Mother would give us the best piece of advice a Mother can give a child, "Find yourself something to do and make yourself happy." So we spent long summer hours playing "house" under the mulberry trees or reading *The Bobbsey Twins*, *Bambi* or *Nancy Drew* while sitting in a mimosa tree. The fluffy pink mimosa blossoms were our fragrant powder puffs while the wild daisy weeds furnished us the yellow eggs and rice for our make believe dinner and the mulberries stained our mouths, feet and fingers as we snacked on the fruit.

We created a world for ourselves and were never bored.

In the Chinese language the word for boredom is made up of two characters, one for heart and one for killing. Can it be that boredom kills the human heart? Nothing appears to kill creativity like boredom, and nothing releases creativity like denying the existence of boredom. For sure, boredom stifles creativity as apathy and lethargy sap energy. And let us be reminded that boredom is a choice even as every day we choose life or death.

Anything that breaks into the routine of daily life can be classified as an adventure. My Nepalese Facebook friend has defined adventure best when he said, "Adventure is an attitude that we must apply to the day-to-day obstacles of life, facing new challenges, seizing new opportunities, testing our resources against the unknown and in the process discovering our own unique potential." Rapendra Maharja . (Facebook)

It is easy to be philosophical about the problems of life but not so easy to apply the attitude of adventure to the obstacles of everyday life. When have you heard someone say, "I'm not having a problem, I am having an adventure?"

Illness is an unknown territory where unknown challenges and opportunities present themselves. My nephew, who is fighting melanoma that has spread to his brain, has the most wonderful attitude. He sees this illness as a learning experience and he will be able to help others when they face a similar experience. In times of adversity and illness, he is discovering his unique potential.

Traditionally we have thought of romance (illicit or not) and travel as two forms of high adventure. We remember with nostalgia a summer romance, while travel to exotic places in real time or in the imagination brings feelings of excited anticipation. People seek adventure vicariously through movies, computer games and novels. Sometimes adventures of fantasy can be the best of all because no demands are made but are only experienced as fun. The movie "Thelma and Louise" ranks as a movie of high adventure. A good novel fulfills the desire to escape into unknown places and experience the story through the personality of another person. Dan Brown's novels, such as the "DaVinci Code," are a perfect example of intrigue and mystery based on legend set in exotic cities. No wonder they have sold millions of copies.

A favorite story of mine is about a relative's grandmother who immigrated to the United States from London with her five-year-old son, in the 1930's. As she was getting settled, she read a notice in the

New York Times that the Princeton Alumnae were holding a reunion in a downtown hotel. Somehow she was able to crash the party, and while she was standing by the punch bowl, met the man who became her second husband. They had a happy marriage and when he died she went to another Princeton reunion and stood by the punch bowl again. While standing there she was introduced to the man who became her third husband. So when we have a goal in mind, my friends and I say that we are going to "stand by the punch bowl." This phrase is a metaphor for seeking allies to help in whatever adventure we engaged. This lady is one of my favorite people I never met because she faced life with a spirit of adventure.

Geneen Roth states my sentiments when she says that chocolate is something you have an affair with, and I agree, especially if it is Belgian chocolate. I could also have an affair with mashed potatoes swimming in butter. Isabella Allende says it best, "You don't have to wait for the perfect companion to have a richly romantic life." To live a deeply romantic life is to have every decision you make on love: self- love, love of others, love of ideas, activities and places, love of smell, tastes, sights, sounds, and textures. Living this way brings romance into the smallest, most ordinary moments and leads to lots of large and extraordinary adventure. Aphrodite: A Memory of Senses.

Sometimes something as ordinary as shopping qualifies as an adventure. The anticipation of the hunt for the perfect antique or funky junk or outfit and persevering to find the treasure through the trials of traffic, disappointment, and tired feet has all the emotions of a Harrison Ford movie without the bad guys and the snakes. Matching wits in bartering and haggling over the price brings a sense of the adventure of one-upmanship, success and triumph. Retail therapy can be a welcome break from the sameness of daily life, and as an antidote to depression, shopping provides a momentary rush of "feel good," until the credit card bill comes due. However, shopping can never be a substitute for living.

We recommend that people live a life of adventure even though the reality is that we live in a very fearful society. We are afraid of strangers and unfamiliar places, so we limit our world to the familiar. The media feeds a constant diet of violence on the morning, noon and evening news, so no wonder we are afraid. The primary example of our societal paranoia is the number of guns we Americans own. Almost everyone I know, men or women, carry a gun. Recently my sister-in–law had a break-in at her home while she was at school. When the local police came, they told her to get a gun. A lot of good that would do. In the first place she was not at home, second, was she supposed to shoot someone and have to live with that memory the rest of her life? She took a much more sensible path and got a garage door and an alarm system.

Life gives us many opportunities to face our fears. Around 1993, my friends were exploring new kinds of adventure so with their encouragement I decided to go to the Florida Keys and swim with the dolphins. I expected a beautiful, exhilarating experience of cross species communication in an exotic tropical setting. Instead I had to face some deeply ingrained fears. As soon as I put on my snorkeling mask and tried to breathe I felt like I was suffocating and became terrified. I became so panicked I could hardly breathe at all. The act of will demanded by the circumstances was almost super human. The memories that arose were of the ether mask that I screamed and fought against when I was 6 years old and my tonsils were being removed.

The experience of being in deep water, with huge animals that wanted to bump and thump me in unexpected places, was a threat to my feeling of security. Instead of a sense of joy and oneness, I experienced a sense of estrangement from the natural world and the spiritual high that I was anticipating became a deep psychological healing of old trauma.

So unexpected adventures can often confront and confound us. For example, my husband always carries a legal hand gun. During his long career as a banker, we learned of area bank robberies and we personally knew a banker and his wife who were kidnapped and locked in the trunk of their car overnight. Criminals now rob convenience stores, but in the late 1980's, they robbed banks. One cold, rainy winter morning, December 31, to be exact, Clyde got to the bank while it was still dark.

After he had parked and was unlocking the back door, a masked man stepped around the corner and accosted him with a deadly weapon. Clyde's arms were full of paperwork he had taken home and table scraps for a Saint Bernard owned by one of his employees. His gun was in his pocket, but he could not get it out. In the fray that ensued he wrestled the man to the ground, and the robber ran away never to be apprehended. As a friend remarked, "Clyde was not about to let anybody takes the bank's money." This story has become a part of our family mythology as all stories of adventures should. Bank robberies aside, just to live is an adventure.

We think of the miracle of conception, and how a microscopic entity joined with another microscopic entity and through nine months of gestation becomes a human being. What an adventure that tiny egg has already been on when it pushes forth through the birth canal and becomes beautiful baby. As Peter Pan says, "To live in the world would be an awfully big adventure."

A fractal of my life adventure began when I was eleven years old and went to church camp for two weeks. I got on a red Trailways bus at the Bus Station in my little town cattycornered across from the Square, (the building is still called the Bus Station even though no busses have run through Colquitt since the 1950s). My Dad owned the bus station so we traveled everywhere on the bus, at half the regular price. The bus drivers were personal friends and took care of my sister and me. At Columbus, GA. the site of Ft. Benning, soldiers were everywhere and I changed buses to go Warm Springs, GA. in the foot hills of the Smoky

Mountains. Warm Springs is the town where Franklin Roosevelt found courage to face his disabilities and embrace the adventure of his life that lead to his presidency of the United States. I had a wonderful two weeks making new friends, swimming in the cold mountain lake and hiking the mountain trails. The fractal that has replayed over and over in my life is one of going into the unknown, not knowing where, or who my traveling companions are, or even why I was going. I say that when a door opens, I walk through it.

People may choose many paths to adventure. All experience is an arch where through gleams that untraveled world whose margins fade forever and forever when I move," Alfred Lord Tennyson said many years ago. No matter the path, reaching beyond ourselves offers opportunity for personal growth through expansion of the mind and brain and give richness to the retirement years. Travel, by taking the country roads and meeting local people, may bring lots of new tales and offers new perspectives.

The next horizon that beacons may be a new field of study that you are curious about, a foreign language, photography, or quantum physics, wood working or snorkeling. The field of interesting things to learn and do is endless for those who want to live a dynamic life. Adventure looms everywhere for those who are determined to grow and not remain static and boring.

In lieu of travel, great adventures of imagination and fantasy happen in the mind. Every invention, every book, every movie was first in someone's imagination. So to day dream is a good thing. We can experience an adventure viscerally when we imagine that we are in the desert with Lawrence of Arabia, and feel the hot desert wind, and smell the camel dung. So, here we go into the unknown.

We can have adventures of the imagination through stories. As children we may have read Alice in Wonderland and dreamed of going down the rabbit hole or visiting the Land of Oz with Dorothy. Perhaps we read about the Knights of the Round Table and King Arthur, or the exploits of Odysseus. As an adult my all-time favorite movie has been Star Wars while my friends favor Harry Potter and Lord of the Rings. In these famous stories we see examples of Joseph Campbell's teaching on "life as a Hero's journey." Through his life-long study of Myth, Campbell saw that each hero in the classical stories followed a similar journey. We can examine our lives and each event in our lives from this rubric.

In Campbell's precept, the call to adventure is the first step, which we can answer or we can reject or ignore. If we do not respond to this demand, it will reappear in another form because it is the Soul's call to fulfill our destiny. If we accept the call, allies will appear to help us and doors will open where there were no doors. But we will still have to go through the dark night of the soul, when we lose almost everything, even our sanity or our life. This trial is faced before we achieve the place of integration or success and become master of two worlds. A life of adventure awaits us as we respond to the call. Mary Oliver reminds us in her poetry, "Do not be content with stories." As Bresny says, "The universe is conspiring to make your life interesting."

The Universe was conspiring to make my life interesting as I waited in the Atlanta airport for my flight and an old friend came up to speak to me. He told me about his latest undertaking which included leaving his recent job to enter the new field of designing holographic images of deceased celebrities. His company designed the incredible lifelike image of

Michael Jackson shown at the Billboard Music Awards. He shared with me his plans to holographicaly re-image Elvis Presley and Marilyn Monroe. He has been approached by the United Nations to do images of five people who changed history to be displayed at the United Nations Headquarters in New York. Needless to say, my imagination was on overdrive as I lived his adventures vicariously.

Living with a sense of adventure can be as simple as smiling and speaking to someone you do not know. As we cross the boundary of otherness, we can make new friends and have stories to share. When we open our mind and heart to new experiences and new people, I call this the hospitality of the open heart. If we befriend someone, preferably a child, show kindness and compassion to another ethnic group or culture, in the process we can grow in our understanding and our world view.

Perhaps we can make a part of our lives a whirligig, the equivalent of the Australian aborigines' walkabout. A walkabout is an opportunity to meander the streets at random, going places you've never been before, having conversations with people you never knew before. Perhaps it will be an opportunity to do some sacred eavesdropping. We can listen with focused attention to the sounds around us, whether they are street sounds or Nature's cacophony. And we can listen to the stories of people's lives as they are lived with high drama.

Recently, as I was waiting at the front door of a downtown hotel for a taxi, the doorman and I started to chat. He was a political refugee from Liberia, and in the course of a five minute conversation, I learned the cause of the Civil War in Liberia that he had escaped with two sons, leaving his wife and other children behind. After only two years in this country he had earned an Associate's degree, and was working on a four year degree in public health. His goal is to reunite his family and to work in his chosen field. I had entered into another's life and was filled with admiration for his journey and with appreciation for the hope that my country offers to refugees. I experienced the joy of the hospitality of the open heart.

The search for Spiritual depth, the longing to connect with the ineffable, to connect with the Mystery may lead to the greatest adventures of all. The adventures of the Spirit are not for the faint of heart.

The pilgrimage called El Camino de Santiago has been the chosen spiritual experience for thousands of pilgrimage since the 1100's. The 500 mile walk is a discipline of self-exploration through the rigors of extreme physical exertion. I have greatest admiration for four friends who have undertaken this trip recently.

The movie *The Way*, starring Michael Sheen, tells the story of a group of pilgrims walking the Camino de Santiago or Way of St. James, and the psychological and spiritual transformations that were the results.

Likewise, In India, thousands of Hindu pilgrims line the banks of the Ganges for a ceremonial baptism, in spite of the cold, polluted water, while hundreds of thousands of Muslims journey to Mecca on the pilgrimage required by their faith. These journeys remind me that the greatest spiritual adventure we can undertake, is to try to ignore the incessant demands of the ego and to live from the heart in the pure love of Christ Consciousness.

Who are the spiritual adventurers you most admire? These are the people who opened the world to another level of unfolding truth. They turn the kaleidoscope of our understanding to show a new and different way of living. I have recently become an admirer of William Wilberforce who, as a Member of Parliament, dedicated his life to outlawing the slave trade in England and by his moral courage changed the public mores of the English people and helped save England from a bloody revolution. He is an example of what one person can do who has answered the call of Spirit. We need people of the caliber of Wilberforce to take on the great issues of our time.

People—whose inner life is manifest in deeds of compassion such as Wilberforce, and contemporary people who lead the environmental, social justice and prison reform movements are the morale barometer of our times.

A dynamic life lived with a spirit of adventure creates a lot of fun.

Go Deeper

○ What color do you think of when you think of adventure? The scene that comes to my mind is Africa: the lush green trees and plants of the jungle, the wild animals lurking everywhere. However, the color I have chosen to represent adventure is rust, the color of transformation. Rust is a combination of the brown color of the earth and the golden color of the sun. When a metal rusts through oxidation it becomes something entirely new. Through an alchemical process metal turns into rust and goes back into the elements. Likewise, adventure can change us, we can have experiences and learnings that give us wisdom and depth. I am thinking of Paulo Coehlo's classic book, *The Alchemist*.

○ What rates as high adventure in your world?

o Do you have a story about an adventure you can share or write in a journal?

o Who is your favorite adventure author?

o What is your favorite adventure movie? I have a crush on Indiana Jones.

o Have you been involved in one of the social or political movements: i.e. ecology, solar energy, fresh food, peace? Write or tell someone how this involvement has changed you.

o Has it given you personal satisfaction and a sense of accomplishment? Or, has it made you suffer from burn-out, bitterness or despair?

Go Lightly

Here are ideas for ordinary adventure right outside your own door.

○ Take a walk around your neighborhood and engage a stranger in conversation. Reach out to a family of another ethnicity and take them for ice cream.

○ For a little while get out of your comfort zone and volunteer in a new setting.

○ Visit a factory or a farm to learn about products we use daily.

○ Sign up for a continuing education class in whatever peaks your interest.

○ Write in a journal about your ordinary every day adventures and how they enriched your life.

Blood Pressure

Her pressure was taken

Her health assured

"Just take this pill every day without fail"

"It will keep hypertension away"

But, the FDA makes us say

At high amounts it caused cancer in rats

In laboratory tests

She took the pills and clutched them softly

"I'll put it where the rats can't get to it," she said.

There's more than one way

To look at everything.

Dr. Ted Ary

FUN

A scene from Swamp Gravy Play "Good Medicine"

by Jo Carson

I ran away from home and got married when I was 13 and we farmed;

And I had his mother and daddy to take care of and pretty soon there were children,

And three meals a day;

And I went to the fields and shook peanuts and hoed peanuts, picked peanuts, shelled peanuts and things like that;

And I had a wood stove to cook on so we had to cut wood—didn't have electricity;

And then we had corn and you had to hoe it and get it off the cob by hand;

And cotton, I had to hoe the cotton, and pick the cotton;

And then there were cows to milk and feed and chickens and pigs and mules to feed;

And the vegetable garden to plant and hoe and food to put up.

We had a lot of fun.

And then we washed our clothes, put them is a wash pot and boiled them,

We didn't have a machine, and hung them up and ironed them with an iron you had to heat on the stove.

Had to make the soap, lard and potash, lye soap. Supposed to take your hide off, but it never did mine.

When we finally got a wash machine, it had a wringer and my cousin about lost her arm in that.

We had fun.

Then every time you'd see a sprig of grass in the yard, you'd take a hoe and dig it out.

You didn't have nothing to cut grass with so you dug it out.

And hay, oh yes, cut hay and bale it and put it up.

And keep the fences up but my husband did that mostly.

And killing hogs for meat come cold weather, and rendering the fat and preserving everything,

You know, salting, and smoking and canning, making souse, whatever. It was usually three or four at a time, once it was a dozen.

We had a lot of fun.

It's just not fun like you have now.

CHAPTER SIX

HAVE FUN

"Dance Like No One is Watching"

The scene entitled "Fun," from the 1994 Swamp Gravy play 'Good Medicine,' is almost verbatim from an oral history interview. The theme of the scene is "It's just not fun like you have today." The scene was staged with elements of fun, anticipation, surprise. Imagine this. The country woman telling the story is holding a live chicken in one hand and a hatchet in the other and the only prop on stage is a chopping block. As she recounts her life of hard work, she intersperses her speech by putting the neck of the live chicken on the chopping block and raising the hatchet as though to cut the chicken's head off, right there on the stage. Over and over she raises the hatchet as the audience holds its breath while waiting to see blood, then she lowers the hatchet and continues her speech. The tension builds with each segment of lines about work until the chicken is released with the final lines, "We had a lot of fun. It's just not fun like you have now."

I am sitting on a balcony on St. Simon's Island on the Atlantic Coast of Georgia, looking down at the Frederica River, as the shrimp boats go out to cast their nets. To me, it doesn't get any better than this. To enter into beauty and let it permeate your whole being with a sense of gratitude, this is pure pleasure. Later, I plan to have fun, when I take a brisk walk under the arching oak trees covered with Spanish moss.

I invite you to think about the difference between pleasure and fun. My definition of pleasure is a quiet enjoyment of a person, place or situation, for instance, a favorite poem, a beautiful sunset, or conversation with a cherished friend. Music gives me great pleasure and I have discovered that singing in the church choir relaxes my body and lifts my spirit. Each person can work out their own definitions of pleasure and fun. Pleasure for you may be having your loved one scratch your back until you fall asleep.

The definition of fun is different for each person. For my friend, Marsha watching her favorite sports team win a close one is her favorite past-time. I love walking on a beach and feeling all the tension leave my body. For others playing with a rock band is a lot of fun or playing an exciting game of tennis. During March and October, when Swamp Gravy plays are performed, I love to go to our town square with my sign announcing "Free Hugs" and see how many free hugs I can give to both women and men. The fun for me is bringing surprise and laughter to strangers and making their trip even more memorable.

Laughter is usually equated with having fun, but it also contributes to staying healthy. Laughter releases tension and the byproduct is not only happiness but also a youthful attitude and appearance. Laughter relaxes the whole body and it can stay relaxed for up to 45 minutes after a good belly laugh. Laughter protects the heart, as well as, boosts the immune system by releasing endorphins. Dr. Patch Adams is a doctor who has devoted his life to helping sick people recover through laughing at his antics as a clown. I am planning to go to clown school when I am 100. I have already ordered my red clown nose and plan to walk in a parade soon and begin to practice my routine.

A new career path has developed around laughter, not only the research done on laughter by scientists, called Gelatology, but trainers can be certified to hold classes on Laughing Yoga. The new field of laughter teaches people how to enjoy life by laughing and how to find humor in everything. While laughing yoga may seem silly at first, when used in a group setting, the laughter breaks down barriers of shyness and releases people to go beyond their comfort zones and be open to new learning.

It is fun to notice the many different kinds of laughter and also notice how and when people laugh. While a smile is the beginning of laughter and brightens everyone's day, the many kinds of laughter can be classified according to their different intensity and the reason for laughing. As you read these different kinds of laughter, imagine them and practice them and feel where they originate in the body. For instance:

- the chuckle, is very quiet, usually when a person is alone.
- the titter, can be classified nervous laugh, usually in a group setting.

- the giggle, is contagious, with others usually of the female sex.
- the chortle is usually loud and from the belly.
- the cackle, so named because it sounds like a hen after she has laid an egg.
- the belly laugh, very funny, from deep in the mid-section of the body.
- the spurting burst, unexpected, usually happens when your mouth is full of water.
- the snicker, a person wants to laugh but not sure if laughter is appropriate
- the guffaw, kin to a belly laugh but not as long in duration.
- the nervous laughter covers feelings of embarrassment.
- the paradoxical laughter, laughter not appropriate to circumstances.
- the courtesy laughter, needs no explanation
- the contagious laughter, loud, boisterous, laugh at laughter.

- the condescending laughter, meant to make others feel inappropriate or inadequate.
- the evil laughter, think of "the joker," plotting murder or mayhem.

The different ways of laughing are associated with the emotions that foster them: relief, mirth, joy, happiness, embarrassment, or apology. One of the joys of female gatherings is the giggling that brings back childhood memories when everything was funny. I remember many fun times when my giggle box turned over and I couldn't stop laughing. I also remember getting tickled in church and the harder I tried to stop laughing the more I laughed. Hee-Hee is called the head laugh and can also be tee-hee, tee-hee, ha-ha is called the heart laugh and ho-ho is called the belly laugh, maybe because Santa Claus' "ho-ho" is from his big belly. A fun exercise would be to practice each of these different laughs and see where in the body it originates and the different emotions it expresses.

Humor is said to be the energetic transfer of information and was so important that a goddess of healing pleasure was revered in many ancient cultures. The earliest known, is the Egyptian goddess called Bast, who was noted as the goddess of protection, pleasure, music and dance. In Greek mythology, Bawdy Baubo, and in Japanese myths, Uzume are goddesses of healing laughter, and sexuality whose names are synonymous with Mirth. (Goddess in Older Women Jean Shinoda Bowen, HarperCollins 2001.)

Baubo and Uzume both came on the scene when the major goddesses, Demeter in the Greek myth and Amaterasu in the Japanese story, were grieving the loss of their daughters and the earth was in darkness. They were able to lift the goddesses out of their depression and re-green the world through their wild antics. Flashing, without any underwear, brought an element of shock, which turned into surprise and then into hilarity. Today we call it 'mooning.' Through jokes, dance, laughter and exposing their private parts they changed the morphic field of grief and depression into one of happiness and fun and the world became fruitful again. Baubo and Uaume brought "healing laughter to a dire situation" as they both lifted their skirts and exposed their vulvas.

These goddesses illustrated the element that surprise, then shock, then hilarity, play in causing laughter. "She cheered the goddess with her bawdy humor". The logo on the Starbuck's coffee was modeled on one of the early images of Baubo, a mermaid showing her hidden parts. This kind of humor lightens the tension and gives people a new perspective. Women who trust and enjoy each-others company can let their hair down, let their risqué side show and experience belly laugh humor. A girl's night out or a bride's bachelorette party can be occasions for the Goddess Bawdy Baubo to show up. But the gathering doesn't have to be bawdy to be fun. I believe every woman has had the experience of laughing so hard she "peed in her pants."

Everyone has a sense of humor and even rats can laugh when tickled but we can't hear them because they laugh at a frequency too high to be heard by human ears. The rats used in the research by Dr. Jaan Panskeep, loved being tickled and would follow the hands of the researcher around the cage asking for more and more. The evidence suggests that the primal laughter and joy generators are in less evolved regions of the brain and implies that all animals like to have fun.

A few cities have innovative ways to encourage their citizens to relax and have fun: for instance, London has bus stops in the form of swings, so you can swing off the frustrations of the day as you wait for the bus. In Vancouver, B.C. a bus stop has a hammock, but you could fall asleep and miss your bus.

Many serious minded people are always looking for 'doom and gloom' and the latest conspiracy theory feeds their energy of "ain't it awful". Sri Aurobindo is quoted as saying "to listen to some devout people, one would imagine that God never laughs." Some people see the glass as half empty, not half full, others see the glass as overflowing, as in Psalms 23, 'My cup runneth over.' Many spiritual leaders, such as the Dali Lama who is noted for his wonderful sense of humor and his hearty laughter, are grounded in the paradox of human existence and the suffering of the world, yet they are able to enjoy fun and laughter.

At the time of retirement we may realize that we have been so focused on career and raising children that we have not allowed much time for pure enjoyment. In fact we may have forgotten how to "let it all go" and have fun.

In order to have fun everyone needs a toy box and a playmate or two. Playmates are very important because they are the friends who are congenial and trusted and who know us and love us in spite of our faults and idiosyncrasies. A toy box can be as big as a recreational vehicle or as small as a box of watercolors. The RV that was my husband's retirement present to himself was named 'Sally Forth' and we made many wonderful trips across the US in our traveling days. A favorite memories took place on a hot summer Saturday afternoon in rural Tennessee. We had visited our daughter in Massachusetts and were on our way home. A deer came running down a hillside and ran into the side of the vehicle, rendering it not drivable. We thought we would have to stay by the side of the road until Monday morning. However, a few miles down the road we discovered a little town whose car dealership was miraculously having a grand opening with balloons and all. Within a few hours our vehicle was repaired and we were on our way toward home and we had participated in the festivities of the small town's open house.

As we grow older we may still want to fulfill some fantasies that we did not have the money or time to explore when we were young and had a demanding job or a young family. Don't worry that friends may think we are having a second childhood or mid-life crisis, just enjoy yourself and buy that red convertible or motorcycle if you want to and can afford the luxury. Just watch out for buzzards. If you want to know the rest of that story, shoot me an email.

Hobbies and collections make up many toy boxes. My collections include green glassware from the depression era that I use for Christmas and special occasions and beaded hand bags first used by the flappers in the 1920s. For many years I have collected folk art and visionary art which is an untrained artist's way of expressing through art their unique view of their religion and their world. Collecting is a way of learning about history, culture and craftsmanship.

Through the years the contents of our toy boxes and our playmates may change as we outgrow some of our interests and pare down some of our unnecessary clutter. A wonderful legacy for our grandchildren is to play and have fun with them, whether throwing a ball in the park or dancing to the music of the cartoons. "We can dance like no one is watching."

A soul nourishing way to have and care for ourselves is to take one day a week for a Sabbath, a day to rest, take stock, slow down and get in touch with the important things in life. I enjoy spending a whole day at our local park, walking, reading and enjoying the beauty of nature and letting my soul catch up with my body.

So as we seek to have fun and live with a spirit of spontaneity, let's joyfully play the game of life.

Go Deeper

When I think of fun I think of *the color pink*, the color of freshness, of pink roses, of sunrises and sunsets. If we can really let go of our ego and our inhibitions and really have fun we can enter a place of innocence and delight.

○ What is your favorite way to have fun? Are movies or music your passion? Do you love dancing or making jewelry, or does golf or pickleball turn you on?

○ What are the things that give you pleasure? Is it curling up with a good book or a lover? Or watching a rainbow or a sunset or the stars on a beautiful night?

○ What is your favorite way of nourishing yourself?

○ Where would you like to spend some time to nourish your soul?

Go Lightly

○ Look at a picture of yourself as a baby and try to recreate that sense of joyful play.

○ Do something completely uncharacteristic of you. For instance, buy a red rubber clown nose and wear it to a public place and have fun.

○ Make a sign that says "free hugs" and take it to a public place and make someone's day.

○ Watch the video on U-tube of twins laughing uncontrollably as their Father makes faces at them.

○ Plant some pink flowers to remind yourself of the beauty of having fun.

PLAY

Taking Off Emily Dickinson's Clothes

First, her tippet made of tulle,
easily lifted off her shoulders and laid
on the back of a wooden chair.

And her bonnet,
the bow undone with a light forward pull.

Then the long white dress, a more
complicated matter with mother-of-pearl
buttons down the back,
so tiny and numerous that it takes forever
before my hands can part the fabric,
like a swimmer's dividing water,
and slip inside.

You will want to know
that she was standing
by an open window in an upstairs bedroom,

motionless, a little wide-eyed,
looking out at the orchard below,
the white dress puddled at her feet
on the wide-board hardwood floor.

The complexity of women's undergarments
in nineteenth-century America
is not to be waved off,
and I proceeded like a polar explorer
through clips, clasps, and moorings,
catches, straps, and whalebone stays,
sailing toward the iceberg of her nakedness.

Later, I wrote in a notebook
it was like riding a swan into the night,
but, of course, I cannot tell you everything---
the way she closed her eyes to the orchard,
how her hair tumbled free of its pins,
how there were sudden dashes
whenever we spoke.

What I can tell you is

it was terribly quiet in Amherst
that Sabbath afternoon,
nothing but a carriage passing the house,
a fly buzzing in a windowpane.

So I could plainly hear her inhale
when I undid the very top
hook-and-eye fastener of her corset

and I could hear her sigh when finally it was unloosed,
the way some readers sigh when they realize
that Hope has feathers,
that reason is a plank,
that life is a loaded gun
that looks right at you with a yellow eye.

Billy Collins

CHAPTER SEVEN

PLAY

"Find yourself something to do
and make yourself happy."

My daughter-in-law, Kim, gets out in 100 degree weather and runs around on black asphalt chasing a ball. Would that be your idea of play and something fun to do? I would think I had died and been sentenced to Hades. But then I was born before the term physical education entered the school curriculum and I have never been enamored of physical activity. Play, like beauty, is in the eyes of the beholder.

Work and play are closely inter-twined. What is play to some is work to others, as in the afore-mentioned tennis games. People whose lives are completely dominated by their work, always retort when questioned or chided, "I enjoy what I do." It is beyond work and has gone into the realm of pleasure. Work that is completely absorbing, that has an element of challenge and discovery could certainly be considered play. "Anything that is creative, spontaneous, joyful is a form of play." To each his own.

For most of us, most of the time, play is what we do to have fun, to bring enjoyment and lightness into our lives. As humans we long to play, we also love to play. Maybe it is horsing around, or playing make-believe or hitting a ball. Favorite ways to play are personal decisions and these decisions change over time as desires, opportunities and physical abilities change.

When children are growing up, throwing a baseball back and forth is a great way to play. Then Little League games consume us with all the competitiveness and stress on children and parents. As we mature, the games are watched on TV and we become couch potatoes and we play vicariously as we watch team sports. We can enter the excitement, struggle, the joy of winning and the agony of losing without moving a muscle.

In 1560, Pieter Bruegel painted a scene of children playing in a medieval courtyard. The painting is called Children's Games and depicts children playing between 90 and 124 (according to who's counting) different games. And guess what? A store-bought toy is not used in any of the games. Before video games and endless commercial entertainment, children invented their own games, using little except their own creativity. How long has it been since you saw a child roll an old tire or a bicycle hoop? As Mr. Rogers points out, play is the work of childhood, as children develop physical skills, try out adult roles and challenge each other.

What is your favorite way to play? We could probably name thousands of different games even before the launch of computer and video games. Card games are a non-threatening way of interacting, but still show skill or dominance. Families share quality time around a board game, jigsaw puzzle or scrabble, as a favorite way to enjoy each other.

One of my favorite ways of interacting with others is by telling stories about the everyday happenings in my life. I live in a very small town of 2,000 people and during a recent weekend I was part of events that made wonderful stories. Friday morning started with the Chamber of Commerce First Friday breakfast for members only. Except the breakfast had an uninvited guest, a local woman who had not taken her medicine and was in the midst of a psychotic episode. It was hard to keep our mind on the speaker when she was entertaining us by taking her wig off and making inappropriate comments. Since I am a former social worker, immediately after breakfast, I went to Mental Health services, only to discover that they could not help her unless she was a danger to herself or others. What a bummer.

Later in the day, a film crew from a National Farm Show interviewed us about Swamp Gravy and using the Arts and Culture for community and economic development. What fun to tell your story on National Television. Then, three brothers from South Florida who had come to Colquitt to hunt deer had spent the night at our local Bed and Breakfast. When they started to check out, one of the brothers was missing. It was later discovered that he was in jail for indecent exposure. I bet they won't come back to Colquitt to hunt. We have a saying, "You can't make this stuff up." That evening I hosted a group of people from Atlanta as they were thrilled and inspired by the Swamp Gravy play," Brothers and Sisters". And this is just the happenings of Friday.

In the above short story, I am recounting events in my life as a way of passing on information; I am building sympathy for the psychotic woman with the hope that more mental health services will become available. I am bragging about my town and I am gossiping and titillating you by telling about the man who winds up in jail. Storytelling encompasses many forms and intentions, some of which are to recount events, to influence, to titillate, to entertain, to gossip, to impress, to complain. Storytelling is a form of high play.

As you have noticed by now, I like to play by telling stories. Are you a teller of tall tales or do you recount the daily happenings of your life by embellishing them and making them more entertaining?

The idea of play is very prevalent in our everyday speech. We play with fire, we play around, we play fast and loose, we play the martyr. These kinds of play denote an element of risk and daring and potential self-destruction. Then in another context, parents used to admonish their children to "play pretty" and a special toy, usually one bought from a store, was a "play pretty."

Play, as defined by Stuart Brown in the book Pronoia, is a spontaneous behavior that has no clear-cut goal and does not conform to a stereotypical pattern. The purpose is simply play itself; it appears to be pleasurable.

Play is born of curiosity. It can be an exploration of our limits and others because to play is to enter another realm of consciousness. We abandon ourselves to the moment whether it is in mild amusement or a belly laugh. We play to relieve the ordinary stresses and to forget the heaviness of everyday concerns.

Play is a dance between people, friends or competitors. My favorite way to play is with the group of friends who meet each Tuesday night to read poetry and chat. The dance is in the conversation about the poetry, or the happenings of our daily lives. In other settings this dance can take the form of one-upmanship as men tease or goad each other to tell the funniest joke or the most outlandish story.

Somewhere along the road of human development we managed to shift play from fundamental to peripheral. But we engage in many forms of play even if we don't recognize it as such.

One of my heroes is Stephen Jepson, whose motto is "Never leave the playground." His website is www.stephen@jepson.com. Though in his 70's he lives to play, by engaging in physically challenging activities that he creates in his own garden. He is getting younger mentally and physically simply through play. He believes that the key to a long and happy life is through play. Howard Thurman reads jokes before going to sleep so that his mind/brain is full of laughter, not the horrors of the eleven o'clock news.

Many forms of play carry sexual overtones such as flirting, which in Japan's Geisha cultures was carried to a high art form. Flirting is defined as: to amuse, to titillate, even to excite. Flirting is a way of interacting that is paying attention to the opposite sex and can be a sign of a special friendship that is non-sexual or a come-on whose meaning is clear.

Sarah Ban Breathnach asks us to remember "the comfort and joy of the imaginary playmate when you were a child. Just because the rest of the world did not see them did not mean he or she was not real." My imaginary playmate was named Deba King and was my constant companion until my sister was big enough to play with me. My favorite game as a child was "dress up." We would raid the closets where the dress-up clothes were kept and search for the special party clothes no longer used, or formals once worn in relative's weddings. Then we would be transported into grand ladies with hats and gloves. I suppose girls experience this kind of transformation now with Barbie dolls.

There is a whole realm of play which as a child we called "play like." Others have called it make believe or pretend.

Maybe you've had an experience of someone making you angry and you lashed out in an uncharacteristic way and you thought "Where did that come from?" Or found yourself dancing and having fun with child- like abandon and you wondered, "Was that really me?" You have tapped into what Jean Houston calls your inner crew.

We have a crew of different personalities that we can call on as we go through our daily lives. My inner crew is made up of an inner comic, a wisdom keeper, a flirt, a mystic, a writer, an organizer, a home maker, a traveler, a matriarch and many others. As we become aware of the polyphrenia of our personalities, we can choose the most appropriate one for each situation. If you have a chore you hate, or a pressing problem, you can engage the help of a chosen personality to get the job done.

Imagine having all the personalities of the Golden Girls available to you. For instance Dorothy is the conciliator, the peacemaker. Sophia is the wise one,

Rose, the heart filled one and Blanche, the sensualist.

Now imagine going grocery shopping and playing with each of these personalities in the store. Rose, asking dumb questions as the clerk rolls her eyes in disbelief. Dorothy is trying to keep everyone focused as she buys items for the party. Sophia is the wild card as she brings memories of fruits and vegetables in the Old Country. Blanche is seeing sexual innuendos everywhere and flirting with the available male staff of all ages.

After all, as Stephen Colbert points out "Life is improvisation" and what is improvisation but play. A theatrical production is called a Play, and is a particular play as explained in a playbill. Theater is perhaps the ultimate form of playing, because the actors lose their own personalities and "play a part."

Swamp Gravy is the name of a twenty-two year old series of original plays based on stories collected from people who live in the Southwest Georgia geography. It fits the larger description of Play, as described below.

Play tests limits many members of the volunteer cast of the Swamp Gravy plays have never acted, some have not seen a play since high school. The limits of their endurance are tested as they rehearse for two months out of the year while maintaining job, home and family life and civic responsibilities.

Play builds trust. The players learn to trust and depend on each other. Each role is double and triple casted to give performers a chance to have some time away. Those who share roles negotiate with each other when they will be absent. The cast knows that they have each other's back and will cover for each other when the memory slips or when there is trouble in a family. They function as a team.

Play is transformative. Storytelling as a form of play is transformative because it takes the teller and the listener into realms of creative imagination and for brief moments they are transported into another time and place. As the volunteer actors enact a character, they become someone else and can mirror a person very different from themselves. They play like or pretend: they take on another persona.

In the Swamp Gravy plays, boundaries are crossed that might not be crossed in the circumscribed arena of everyday life, new friends are made, new talents are discovered, a new sense of self is discovered that is exciting and engaging.

A good play shows the audience something profoundly

human. Recently I saw a play based on a book called, *Wildflowers in the Median*, written by an elderly woman named Agnes Furey and an incarcerated man named Leonard Scoven. Agnes' daughter and grandson were murdered by Leonard. The book and the play tell the story of the heartbreak of the Mother and the agony caused by child abuse and drug abuse that led to the murder. In an attempt to understand the "Why" of the murders Agnes reaches out to Leonard. Through many conversations a story of restorative justice unfolds. We see the profound humanity of Agnes and Leonard in their relationship with each other. Agnes, though in her eighties, and Leonard, from his prison cell, are pioneering work around restorative justice in many states.

Go Deeper

○ What is your favorite toy box? Is it a tool box, a jewelry box, a tackle box, a box of art supplies or a box at a sporting event? Maybe it is a music box or a musical instrument like John Denver's g uitar.

○ John Denver's line from his song "sunshine on my shoulder makes me happy" reminds us that the color yellow makes us happy. Playing is a way to create happiness. So yellow is the color I have chosen to symbolize play.

○ Where is your favorite playground? Is it a jogging trail or a gym, or a board walk across beautiful wetlands?

○ Do you have animals that are a source of amusement and amazement for you? Do you like to entertain your friends with stories about their antics?

○ What sub personalities make up your inner crew? Do you have a judge, a boss, a glamour girl, a dancer, a dreamer? Can you call them to help when you have a problem?

Go Lightly

○ Greet the sun in the morning and appreciate the myriad ways we are indebted to its rising each day.

Cheer people up by wearing a sunshine yellow shirt.

○ Try making a collection of jokes to share with the elderly or with children. Knock-knock jokes are a great way to play with children.

○ Take a child to an amusement park and ride the merry-go-round or roller coaster with them.

○ Surprise a special person by telephoning them and singing "I just called up to say I love you."

○ Draw a picture of a sunflower with your face in the middle of it.

GRAMMAR

Maxine, back from a weekend with her boyfriend,
smiles like a big cat and says
that she's a conjugated verb.
She's been doing the direct object
with a second person pronoun named Phil,
and when she walks into the room,
everybody turns:

some kind of light is coming from her head.
Even the geraniums look curious,
and the bees, if they were here, would buzz
suspiciously around her hair, looking
for the door in her corona.
We're all attracted to the perfume
of fermenting joy,

we've all tried to start a fire,
and one day maybe it will blaze up on its own.
In the meantime, she is the one today among us

most able to bear the idea of her own beauty,

and when we see it, what we do is natural:

we take our burned hands

out of our pockets,

and clap.

Tony Hoagland

CHAPTER EIGHT

CONVERSE

"I could tell you if I want to, who I really am, but I don't really want to, and you don't give a damn."

"I think I will live and die and no one will ever know what I am like on the inside." When a friend said this many years ago, while in the agony of a bad marriage, I thought it was one of the saddest things I had ever heard. We all live in existential loneliness and we long to share with another from the depth of our being, but it is very rare. True friends speak from an open heart to an open heart. This longing is best expressed by people searching for their soul mate whom they think will be the perfect companion and lover.

I learned a lot about conversation recently when a party was given in my honor in a distant state. A small group of close friends of the host were invited to meet me. Once introductions were made and hands shaken, I might as well have become invisible. The group talked about their mutual friends, children and activities and no one asked me a question about where I lived, how long I was staying or anything else. I might as well have gone to bed. They could have said, "How do you like our city?" "Are you enjoying your grandchildren?" And they would have opened the floodgates of stories from me; their loss, too bad.

When have you had an experience like this? How have you broken through so that you could be a part of the give and take of sharing? This experience made me wonder why meaningful conversation is so hard? Is it shyness or lack of genuine interest or are we too inhibited to reach out to another person?

A scene in the movie "While You Were Sleeping" is etched in my memory, and I laugh every time I think about it. While the main character is in the hospital in a coma, the family has gathered around the dining table to share a meal and to console each other. However, each person is engrossed in his own conversation unaware that no one else is listening, much less following what he is saying. One person is talking about the sick man and his medical regime, another about relatives who are not there, another is talking about the food, another is talking about the trip into the city. There is lots of chatter but no communication, no listening, therefore no interaction. This scene is pathetic because it is so true to life. In contrast, we can experience the ritual of the dining table, where, with congenial friends, we engage in a sharing of unhurried time, of mutual concerns and caring. Even if no serious subjects are broached, the gentle flow and give and take of talking and listening brings a deep sense of comfort.

We simply want to know that we are seen and heard. Conversation can consist of blah, blah, blah, or can be real dialogue or at least attentive listening.

Conversation is a basic level of communication. Peggy Rubin, in her book, "To Be and How To Be," has said that the point of the spoken word is to change the Universe. How do we change the Universe when we speak? What are the words that we can say that will or could change a person's way of seeing the world of nature and their place in it? A level of trust is required to speak from an open heart and to speak with intention and focus. Even if we are not heard, the vibration of our voice changes the universe. After all, in the Old Testament God spoke the Universe into being. The spoken word is powerful and once spoken cannot be recalled. James O'Dea says that we are "called to make every point of contact with others a quality connection. Everyone counts in your quest to humanize the world."

What are the elements of a good conversation? Do you agree that conversing consists of give and take, mutual attentiveness and respect, and active listening? We long to share at the intellectual level, the friendship level and the heart level. A good conversation is also marked by laughter, an appreciation of the irony, the pathos of the human condition.

As we get older we get habituated to expecting people to say certain things or speak in certain ways. Nag, shrew, complainer, braggart are names for people who use their voices to express their frustrations and dissatisfactions. They are so engrossed in their narcissistic world that they turn everyone off and wonder why they are avoided. Our family and friends accuse us of telling the same stories called "war stories," over and over. And so we begin to talk only about the weather, or the news, or the price of gas.

Conversation consists of "Hello, How are you? What's the news? How is your family?" Personal day-to-day issues and problems are our chief concerns. Venting to an understanding ear helps us to hear ourselves and can become a kind of therapy. How can we break out of these habits and engage in life-affirming conversation?

Eleanor Roosevelt has said, "Great minds discuss ideas, average minds discuss events, small minds discuss people." Is your mind great, average or small? Where does your conversation fall? Do you love discussing ideas? Sometimes we want to talk about ideas and share some exciting topics of research or a book we are reading or an interesting movie that made us think. These conversations can be stimulating and lead to learning from another's perspective. Any topic can be discussed from the standpoint of an abstract idea, a present or past event, people's involvement or accomplishments. For instance: the topic of sex trafficking can be explored as an idea, where and when did it start, where is it most prevalent. Also it can be discussed from the standpoint of a particular event and the involvement of people who are trying to change this world wide scourge.

The latest interesting and stimulating conversations are around consciousness and the evolutionary impetus that is the next frontier of inner space.

Most of my acquaintances want to talk about events or people. Fewer are willing to talk about ideas. When is it appropriate to talk about people? What differentiates gossip from sharing information about friends or acquaintances? When is gossip harmful? It is all about our intention. Talking about other people is harmful when the intention is to titillate, or to feel superior, or to take pleasure in another's bad luck.

I've always had a question about gossip because my Mother told me everything. For instance, when I was a young teen, she pointed out to me the woman that was her brother's Mistress, so I did not grow up to be naïve about the ways of the world and I am grateful.

Conversation can be bonding or divisive: i.e., if political discussion can be maintained at the idea level and not allowed to deteriorate into personal attacks and accusing opponents of being un-American. Rather, it can be a sharing of perspectives and a learning experience for all concerned. Disagreement and conflict can be productive, but only if marked by real discourse and seeking a middle ground of mutual respect. Discussing sports can be a bonding experience between grandparent and grandchild and make for happy memories and can be explored at the level of idea, event or sports celebrities.

Problems in conversing may have to do with the fact that we don't know how to listen. Our culture is inundated with noises that are jarring and invasive. We are so accustomed to sounds that we keep a radio or TV turned on because the quiet makes us feel lonely. We have forgotten what quiet sounds like. (Remember the 1960's song "The Sound of Silence".) We are so busy we don't want to be interrupted by listening to someone's recitation of their day, unless of course, it is very funny. Because we have been taught that multi-tasking is good, we are always half listening while we do something else and consequently listening has become a lost art.

Ernest Hemingway pointed out that most people never listen. We do not give attention to the other person to hear what they are saying because we are busy thinking about what we are going to say in response. A recurrent problem for me is that many people don't let me finish my thought, much less my sentences before they interrupt with their own responses. Julian Treasure helped me to understand this situation by pointing out (on You Tube) that men are acculturated to listen in order to solve a problem as quickly and efficiently as possible. They get right to the point and the conversation is over. Sometimes they try to solve the problem and only make it worse. In my experience, women interrupt because they are anxious to share a story from their experience or an idea pertinent to the discussion. At any rate it is a subtle, unconscious way of discrediting another.

Some ways to cultivate listening skills are listening consciously, listening actively and listening with compassion. Conscious listening requires us to retrain the brain to listen to the quiet by taking time to be in a silent space, and from the silence, we can listen to the voice of intuition, guidance, angels, the Holy Spirit and give our soul an opportunity to grow.

When we listen actively we notice body language, mood, pitch of voice, nervousness and engage with our whole awareness in attentiveness. We listen for what the person is really saying. We wonder why they have mentioned this particular topic. How is the body language contradicting what is being said? Is the person sitting with arms folded, kicking and swinging a foot as though to kick a person and avoiding eye contact?

The highest level of listening is compassionate listening with an open heart and with full attention, without criticism or judgment. To listen with compassion means without interruption or advice giving or saying "I know" because you don't know what another person is experiencing. Compassionate listening shows the person that you care, you really do care.

If you want to have good conversation find a quiet place like a restaurant or a car where you can see each other face to face; a quiet place in nature opens us up to the beauty of the surroundings to delight in deep sharing with another. When you make eye contact and give undivided attention by leaning forward, you signal that you are really listening. You can make agreements with the person that you want to have a talk with, such as no complaining, no "ain't it awful" stories, no debates, and no one-upmanship stories.

Casual conversation around a sensitive issue can be based on spoken or unspoken agreements. One of the agreements might be that the conversation can be changed or stopped if it becomes uncomfortable for either party. I often quote Forrest Gump, "That's all I have to say about that." You can also change it to say, "That's all I want to say about that." By summarizing what the person is saying or by asking questions for clarity or for feedback you can make sure you understand and you can gauge where the person is hurting. Then ask leading questions, what happened next or what is the rest of the story?

According to your history with the person you can gauge the depth of the conversation, after all, it is not therapy and definitely not for advice giving but for sharing of mutual support and love. We listen with empathy and compassion, we signal "I not only see you, I feel your pain." We listen for the larger story that is being lived out. How can we help a person see their life as a larger story and not be caught up in the pain and drama of the moment? In what way is the friendship or relationship a part of the larger story?

Communion is the ultimate goal of conversation and intimacy is another name for communion. The way to intimacy is through vulnerability by speaking what your heart tells you to say. Speaking from an open heart, an understanding and non-judgmental heart is a mark of true friendship. When you take a chance and risk being real, conflict can arise. We are afraid of conflict and will do almost anything to avoid it since we don't want to rock the boat. Sometimes we need to rock the boat so that a new direction can be set. Conflict changes the dynamics and opens the conversation and the relationship to new levels of understanding.

When was the last time you had a good fuss with your significant other? How did it change your interactions and expectations? How did it lead to a new level of intimacy? When two people relate to each other with authenticity and humanity, God is in the electricity that converges between them.

When was the last time you spoke truth to power? Was it when you spoke at a public hearing to express your opinion as a concerned citizen? Have you had an opportunity to share your wisdom with a person you consider powerful in the political or social arena? Screwing up your courage to speak your truth is a personally liberating "rite of passage." My friend died unexpectedly and left his wife with a business that she knew nothing about managing. She knew that if she turned it over to their son the business would suffer a disaster. She was able to assert her truth and risk alienating her son. Thankfully she taught herself what she needed to know and successfully managed the business until she was able to sell it for a nice profit.

As we age, real conversation becomes even more important. This time of life affords us the opportunity to learn the skills of conversation, such as the ability to ask for what we need and want, to ask for help and be willing to receive it when it is offered. These conversational skills may have been learned along the way but are critical as we establish agency in the years of retirement. It is easy to give up a sense of agency and feel that we have to bow to our children's desires about our life. What we really want is to claim our power and chart the course of our life and be the person we have always known we are.

Another level of communication is through story. From earliest times cultures have communicated history and values, trials and triumphs through story telling. The Greek theatre was designed to provide an opportunity for dialogue about what was important to the community. Since 1992, the Arts Council of the little town where I live, Colquitt, GA., has presented an original play each year based on the stories of the local citizens. The plays transmit the values of the rural South Georgia people.

The heritage of story-telling has been handed down from our Scotch-Irish ancestry. In Swamp Gravy we have a saying "You can't make this stuff up." The stories are so entertaining and compelling that we understand the truth is stranger than fiction. Another memorable quote form Swamp Gravy is "Northerners tell stories and call it therapy; Southerners tell stories and call it swapping lies." Swapping lies is a form of entertainment: of telling jokes, of one-upmanship, of telling cultural truths in a light, conversational way usually to a rapt audience of friends or admirers.

We simply want to know that we are seen and heard when we are engaged in conversation. Conversation, dialogue, communication then communion are progressively deeper levels of sharing through speech. In the Christian tradition Communion is the ritual of the bread and wine which unites the congregant with the Source. Common Union is the ultimate goal of conversation, and is considered a meeting of minds and hearts, a mystical attunement on the soul level.

As we get clarity about the quality of our conversation and desire for intimacy and communion with our loved ones, we are ready to move to another level and unpack the garbage in our lives and relationships, but first let's go deeper and lightly.

Go Deeper

In your tool box I hope you have a "talking stick." The talking stick is from the Native American tradition and is a ceremonial object passed from person to person when in Council. It allows each member present an opportunity to share their Sacred Point of View.

○ When and where have you been in a social situation and found conversation very difficult? Why did you find it so?

○ How many people do you talk to in a week? Is your conversation satisfying or just a lot of words?

○ What has been a recent memorable conversation? Heard any good stories lately?

Who is your trusted friend with whom you can share ideas, dreams and hopes?

Go Lightly

○ When you are serving on a committee you might consider using a talking stick to ensure that every voice is heard.

○ Make the day of a person at a check-out counter by giving them a sincere compliment. "You are so nice, pretty, efficient, etc."

○ Say words that change the Universe to a loved one, "I love you", "I am sorry", "Please forgive me".

THIRST

Another morning and I wake with thirst
For the goodness I do not have. I walk
out to the pond and all the way God has
given us such beautiful lessons. Oh Lord,
I was never a quick scholar but sulked
and hunched over my books past the
hour and the bell; grant me, in your
mercy, a little more time. Love for the
earth and love for you are having such a
long conversation in my heart. Who
knows what will finally happen or
where I will be sent, yet already I have
given a great many things away, expect-
ing to be told to pack nothing, except the
prayers which, with this thirst, I am
slowly learning.

Mary Oliver

CHAPTER NINE

UNPACK

"We carry around lots of worldly baggage."
Jo Carson, playwright of the Swamp Gravy play
"Good Medicine"

The word baggage carries the connotation of an excessive amount of something. Women carry huge purses with everything they "might" need on a trip around the world and they weigh enough to cause back problems. We also carry baggage of grudges, betrayals, anger and much more.

The word baggage is a great metaphor for the excess of personal belongings we have but also for charged emotional issues we carry. In her play, Jo Carson equates healing with recognizing and clearing the body of its excess of emotional baggage. When we unpack a suitcase after a trip, we take each item out, examine it to determine whether it needs to be cleaned, then put it in its proper place.

At the approach of retirement age, we can examine our life for the physical and emotional encrustations that hold us back from living the dynamic life intended for us.

We may realize that we are surrounded by the accumulated possessions of a life time. "He who dies with the most toys wins," is a true mantra of our time. We have been brainwashed to believe that we are defined by our stuff and our life has value according to how much stuff we have. We deplete the earth's non-renewable resources through our insatiable appetites for junk to fill our ego needs. We have too many possessions, too many choices of what to wear, what to eat, where to travel, how to be entertained. Our possessions have become our security blanket, we can enjoy them but they can cause us stress. We dread cleaning because we have too much stuff, and even though we love our old junk, it is an emotional drain on our psyche. We have fallen victim to advertisements which tell us that we will be happy and fulfilled if we only buy the right car or use the right anti-aging face cream, ad nauseum. Friends, who were chided by their children to start cleaning out, throwing away the accumulations of 60 years of marriage, told them to burn the house down when they die, so they won't have to sort through and get rid of stuff. What a waste that would be.

I confess that books are my security blanket and are on the list of necessities for my life. My husband told me that I was trying to read myself into heaven. I would be so happy with a house that was nothing but bookshelves and I could read every one. My fantasy is that I could stow away in a Barnes and Nobles, drink coffee and read. Anyone want to join me there in never, never land?

The TV show "Hoarders" has touched some deep feelings. Many people feel secure only if they have lots of material possessions, maybe because they experienced poverty as a child or come out of a fear mentality of 'I might need it later'.

We also keep things far beyond their usefulness because we are sentimentally attached to them. They hold precious memories for us and if we discarded them we would feel as though we dishonored the past. For instance, I still have my wedding dress and the coat I wore to New York on my honeymoon sixty years ago. Hoarding can also be a habit handed down in the family or an antidote to boredom and depression.

We don't have to wait until we move to a different home, to get rid of items we have outgrown either physically, mentally, emotionally or spiritually. We can pare down and not feel so bogged down. Thank goodness for thrift stores and Good Will that can re-use and re-purpose our cast offs. The old saying, "One man's junk is another man's treasure" never is more true than at a thrift store. When we know that our unused items will help someone else, discarding them is easier. Volunteers from our church run a thrift store which recycles good clothing and household items. From the sale of items priced for 25 cents to $4.00 enough money is raised to fund a food bank which provides groceries to 400 families per month.

At the other extreme are obsessive compulsive people who don't keep anything. I admire people who can get rid of things they no longer need or use. And the treasures they choose to keep are so well organized: the pictures are in albums; the letters and cards from loved ones are neatly saved; the house is always neat; and the pantry is in order. Too bad I did not get any of this gene. Most of us fall somewhere between these two extremes. Where on this continuum from hoarder to 'trasher' are you, and in which direction do you feel you need to move? I just made up the word 'trasher'. Do you know a person that will put your half-full soft drink in the trash before you have time to finish it, or discard an important newspaper article that you were hoping to read later? Who can forget Jack Nicholson's portrayal of an obsessive, compulsive man in the movie, "As Good As It Gets?" I wish I could find a happy medium between the hoarder and the 'trasher' and become a minimalist keeping only what is absolutely necessary for my life.

Retirement is a good time to take stock of our physical possessions as well as our emotional blocks and burdens. These are the years when we can recreate ourselves and move into a different phase of life. In order to live dynamically it behooves us to unpack our worldly baggage. Imagine the burden of baggage that is too heavy. We feel the stress in our arms, back, shoulders and neck when we carry a heavy bundle. Our bodies cry out also when we carry emotional burdens such as guilt and sadness over a divorce, a child who has disappointed us, or an unwise decisions that we made. We may feel the tension in our stomach or our skin or in our spine.

The emotional burden of unresolved family conflict is very heavy. We all know families who haven't spoken for many years after a family feud or a dispute over inheritance. Our emotional baggage weighs us down with emotional pain, and many times excess body weight is armor against feeling this emotional pain and can lead to flatness of personality, lethargy and depression.

We are also burdened down by unresolved issues and memories, and old emotional habits. This time of life affords us the opportunity to look back with fresh eyes and make decisions about how we want to live the rest of our life. We can choose to make peace with old painful memories, old hurts. We can let go of people and situations who take up space in our heads and hearts which I call energy vampires. They drain us of vital life force which we can give to other people and events. We can forgive those who have hurt us and those who don't recognize their contribution to our pain.

Then there are some people who are living with emotional baggage, acting out of old wounds. These issues call for help from a trained counselor or therapist and require intense introspection and work. Are you still nursing the wounded child? Tell him to "get over it." Is a rebellious teen-ager still part of your inner crew and shows her (or his) nasty side sometimes? Are you a rebel without a cause? Sometimes people have a chip on their shoulder because they had to earn their living the hard way and did not inherit money or status? The green-eyed monster of jealousy can rear its head as they see others who seemingly had an easier time and were born with more advantages.

Sometimes we live our lives caught in the past or in the expectation of others. The movie "Shirley Valentine" portrays a woman who broke out of the role of living her family's expectations of a good wife and mother. She kicked the traces and ran away to Greece to everyone's surprise. This movie portrayed the fantasy that many women would like to experience, if they were brave enough.

The nursery rhyme, "I have a little shadow that goes in and out with me," is true for adults and for children. Our shadows are the parts of our psyche, the unrecognized parts of ourselves, that we deny yet project on to others. As my friend says, "Don't bother looking in my closet for my skeletons. They are all over my life."

In the therapy called transactional analysis, popular in the 1970s we learned a term called collecting brown stamps. The brown stamps are old hurts, judgments, slights that we have not forgiven or forgotten or dealt with and are saved and cashed in as grudges, hurt feelings or revenge. Brown stamps are unconscious emotional responses that need to be recognized for what their roots, unpacked and thrown in the garbage.

The struggle to make decisions and to take responsibility for decisions once made can be a shadow. One of the most important tasks of life is to learn to decide, instead of wallowing in indecision and procrastination. Untold energy is wasted as we struggle to make a decision. Asking ourselves a simple question, "What is the worst thing that can happen?" often brings clarity to a choice.

Once a decision is made, there is a sense of relief as we are free to live with the consequences, which many times is easier than deciding. Even when a decision is made that is not healthy or in our best interest the path unfolds and each step of the way we can make new decisions. The path then can become one of learning and mastery.

Instead we have the tendency to blame other for or bad decision, "the devil made me do it", or to live with debilitating guilt which drains our psychic energy. Whatever we hold onto, that we need to let go of, always ends up hurting us. Margaret Mead called clearing these burdens out "freedom from load."

Long held attitudes abound in religion, in government and politics. I am only advocating that we examine them for their helpful life-giving forces or their contracting, numbing qualities. Do they enable us to live a life of love and to show love in its manifold expressions? Are our cherished political beliefs and religious practices based on teachings that have become outmoded by changing times and changing world? Are there sacred cows that we refuse to look at? As you examine a cherished belief, ask yourself if you still believe it. Clearing the past makes room for the new and is part of our evolutionary journey.

We turn a blind eye to those shadow parts of ourselves

and project them on to those nearest to us. Everything can be carried to the extreme even our good intentions. As you consider that our weaknesses are our strengths in excess, I challenge you to think of your greatest strength and examine whether this strength is also your greatest weakness when taken to the extreme. A person who is so helpful, always there when they are needed, can quickly become a martyr neglecting their health in the excess of caring for others.

My strength is that I have no need to be in control of my family or situations, I do not need to have my own way. I am a conciliator, control is not my issue but it quickly becomes an attitude of 'laissez fare' and situations arise when it would be in my best interest to be more assertive even though to do so will produce conflict. I have learned the value of conflict from Peggy Rubin in her book, "To Be and How to Be." So I am more able to face issues and bring them to a head by allowing space for them to surface and find resolution.

Repressed feelings and the need for open disagreement can manifest in physical signals. We have all been in a situation and noticed a person swinging their foot as someone talked to them. We note that the impulse of the foot swinger is to kick the person or at least run away. When we find ourselves swinging our foot, it is interesting to look deep within and explore the real feelings behind the gesture. Also, another common body signal is to sit with arms tightly folded across the chest, which can signal hostility or at least disapproval. The study of body language has become well known and as we become aware of our own body language we can learn about our repressed emotional baggage.

Another way to learn more about ourselves is to look at the traits and values handed down through our families. Some families have prejudices against people of another race or ethnic group that are passed down through the generations. Sensationalism of the news media revives racial and ethnic prejudices by focusing on the current riot, or terrorist attack without educating the viewers on the history of abuses that led to the radicalization of the attacker.

The love of sports and physical activity may be a bond across generations in your family. What are the traits of character handed down in the family which have influenced your choices? What are the values that have come down from your parents and grandparents? In some families a clan like commitment to each member of the family group is a motivating force. What would you say is the guiding value handed down in your family which you have tried to pass on to your children?

Maybe honesty in business and personal relations, is a

227

strong family value. The freedom to explore new ideas, or countries or endeavors may be encouraged. Friendship or care for the earth, or an appreciation of the beauty of the outdoors, or artistic pursuits or music, or the beauty of words and reading may be strong values in your family. My family has always valued education, especially the education of women. My daughter is the 4th generation of women in our family to graduate from college, going back to my Grand Mother attended college in the 1870s when the South was still devastated by the ravages of the Civil War and 50 years before women had the right to vote.

What are the family stories of kinship, family scandals, heroic deeds which hold our family values and that need to be shared with the next generation? I take pride in telling my grandchildren about their great grandfathers. My husband's father was born in 1900, had little opportunity for formal education and started to work as a young teen ager to help support the family. He was recognized for his brilliance and opportunities were opened to him. He lost everything in the crash of 1929, rebuilt his life and was widely respected for his business acumen and philanthropy when he died at age 90. My father helped to pay his way through the University of Georgia working for the Georgia Power Company by installing electric wiring and bringing the convenience of electricity to the rural farms. He was in the first graduating class in Agricultural Economics at the University of Georgia and was a consultant to farmers all his working life.

The family values that have passed down through many generations are: hard work; education; determination; and true grit; coupled with commitment to family, church and community. When we recount a family story, and rehearse our values, we turn the kaleidoscope of understanding and new colorful personalities are revealed.

Most of us go through life worried, restless, and fretful, about our duties, responsibilities that claim our time and attention. As Boomers, perhaps the time has come to lighten up, unpack the burdens of too much stuff, as well as the emotional baggage of unresolved conflict and guilt. The attitudes that no longer serve us can be released and the family stories that have shaped us can be celebrated.

We can become lighter as we prepare to celebrate the gift of our one amazing life.

> *Hafiz says: "when the violin*
> *Can forgive the past,*
> *It starts singing.*

We can sing because we are free to become fully ourselves and to bring our gifts without our baggage to serve the world.

Go Deeper

Brown paper bags are widely recognized as the symbol of Bloomingdale's department store.

○ From your storage box choose some brown paper bags to use as we unpack and discard.

○ Are you carrying baggage that is too heavy?

○ Where in your body do you feel stress?

○ Is it in your stomach, your back, your skin?

○ What part of your anatomy responds to emotional stress and worry?

○ Who do you need to forgive?

○ Take a quick mental scan of your home and think about the items you need to pitch, or give away or recycle.

○ Imagine yourself throwing some of these into the brown paper bags and dropping them in a donation bin.

○ Make a list of what you need beyond food, clothing and shelter?

○ Are music, beauty and friends on the list? What would you hate to live without?

Go Lightly

○ How can you simplify your life?

○ Develop the habit of discarding something each time you bring something new into your home.

○ Lie on the grass and think about what you will carry with you when you return to the brown earth.

○ Go and dig a deep hole in the earth and bury all the hurts from the past, say a blessing over them and leave them for nature to recycle.

○ Imagine yourself a balloon, floating weightless and free.

Liberating a Made-up Mind

As I walk into the room,
The door slams shut behind me.

The darkened room in front of me is filled
With red Day–Glo signs.

DON'T/STOP

SHOULD/NO

SHOULD NOT

BE QUIET/BE GOOD

DON'T MOVE/DON'T MOVE

DON'T BREATHE

What are the consequences of not obeying?
A sign in bold black letters informs.

Abandonment

Seventy years later
I open the door and
Dance
Into the sunlight.

A FREE WOMAN

Pat Pothier

CHAPTER TEN

CELEBRATE

Did I live, Did I Love, Did I Matter

Brandon Burchard

The song "Celebration," popular in 1960's is still a fun song, and its message is a reminder to celebrate life. A life review is about making meaning of the experiences and the challenges, seeing the big picture and celebrating. Life can be like a big jigsaw puzzle as we look back, try to fit all the pieces together and make a coherent picture of it. Unfortunate events occur and we are devastated but then with the passage of time we realize that good can come out of the worst of times. We can reframe our life experiences when we look at life as a whole piece. We can become reconciled with life and make peace with the good, the bad and the ugly. We can forgive and be forgiven. "We've all got something to brag, we've all got something to hide," as the Swamp Gravy storytelling song reminds us. We all want and need a reason to celebrate…

Life happens almost without our noticing, and we may need to remind ourselves of the journey. Self-reflection is an important human attribute so "sit back and feast on your life" as the poet Derek Wolcott invites us. A feast is spread before us as we remember our journey and the stories that make it interesting.

The storytelling song which opens and closes each Swamp Gravy performance reminds us, "You've got a story and I've got a story, we've all got a story to tell." My interest in story started in 1991 with the advent of an oral history based theater project called Swamp Gravy in my home town. During the 21 years of listening and recording people's stories, it has been a revelation to me that the simple act of listening to a person's life story validates, gives meaning and empowers the story teller. I had never been interested in people's personal reflections but during my career as a social worker and nursing home consultant I had been troubled as I read the social history in patients' charts. The sketchy information of birth, marriage, children and work left me feeling sad. Where were the stories of their lives, the accomplishments, and the beauty of the human experience? Nothing in the charts reflected the richness, the joys and sorrows, of the people now facing the last stages of their lives.

I have also learned in the process of 21 years of story gathering and listening, that stories we are shaped by the stories that tell ourselves about our lives. The stories that we read as children, or movies, or Super Heroes that shaped our self-story. What is the overarching story or myth of your life? Did you live out of the Cinderella story waiting for your prince to come? Or have you been Little Red Riding Hood and liked to flirt with danger? Do you have friends who are like Sleeping Beauty and try to avoid life by taking to their bed? Or perhaps you know someone like Peter Pan who lollygags around and doesn't want to grow up. I think my story has been "The Little Engine that Could" and its guiding principle, "I think I can, I think I can." Maybe I am the victim of a savior complex, a Super Hero called upon to right all the problems of the world.

Every ancient civilization has gods and goddesses who carry the myths of the culture's religion. These archetypical figures are codes for human experience and religious longing. White Buffalo Calf Woman of the Lakota people is said to have given the Lakota their rituals and ceremonies. Pele, the volcano and fire goddess of Hawaii has been worshipped longer than any other ancient religious figure according to Wikipedia. Maybe because her active powerful presence is very evident in the active volcano on the big island of Hawaii. The ancient stories and myths that have come down to us from Greece carry the potent energies of the stories that one were and are always happening. The Mother and Daughter story of Demeter and Persephone is being re-enacted repeatedly during our time as our daughters are falling into the underworld of addiction and mothers are descending into that world to try to bring their children back into the world of light and love. The goddess Hestia lives on in the love of home and family. Aphrodite is the energy of beauty, sexuality and sensuality. Athena is known for her intelligence, for her love of arts and literature, the love of crafts and skills which make community possible. Sophia whose name means wisdom, is the ancient symbol of the feminine face of God. And on and on. These archetypical attributes are encoded in us and are part of our DNA.

We live out of our self-story because our stories tell us who we are. My Mother was a beautiful, witty woman but her self-story was "I washed my education down the kitchen sink". Some live out of the self-story, "I am sick, I am uneducated, I am poor, I am unlucky. I am a victim of fate or the economy, or my parenting. If only things had been different." But the flip side is, people who tell themselves the story," I am healthy, I am lucky, I am strong" live a self- fulfilling prophesy and are better able to cope with whatever life brings them. We can sometimes live out of our parent's expectations of us (he will never amount to anything) and our own inner guidance (I will show them) and other stories we tell ourselves about our lives. In the Movie, Les Miserables, the poignant song, "Who Am I" was sung by Jean Val Jean when he was seen only as a convict, not as a human being. On a happier note, when my grand-daughters, Carly and Joanna were in kindergarten they had a teacher who called her students "Mrs. Taffets' geniuses" and gave every child a T-shirt proclaiming that they were Mrs.Taffets' geniuses. If every child lived out of the self-story that he was a genius, this world is a very different place. Teachers are second only to parents in formulating the self-story that we carry all of our lives.

Many screens are helpful as we look back at our lives. Life can be reviewed as a journey full of experiences and stories, bends and turns, ups and downs, detours, happiness and sadness and a popular image of the journey of life is the labyrinth. The image of the labyrinth comes from Greek mythology, specifically the story of the Minotaur, half man and half bull, who was imprisoned by King Minos in a labyrinth. Theseus, the hero, is determined to kill the Minotaur and Ariadne, his lover, gives Theseus a ball of twine to mark the path so that he can find his way out. This story is one of tragedy, betrayal and heartbreak but the image of the labyrinth as a metaphor for life abides with us. As we walk a labyrinth we are re-living of the crooks and turns of life and we realize again that we take three steps forward and two backward. We are reminded while that the path is never straight, but full of surprises, all paths lead to the Center where God is.

Many churches have labyrinths which are available to the public. Possibly, the most famous labyrinth, built in the 1200s, is at Chartres Cathedral in France. Grace Cathedral in San Francisco is the site of another well-known labyrinth and Lauren Artress, Dean of Grace Cathedral, has written a book about walking the labyrinth named "Walking a Sacred Path: Rediscovering the Labyrinth as a Sacred Tool."

The labyrinths were first built in cathedrals so that devoted Christians in the middle ages could make a symbolic pilgrimage to Jerusalem when the actual journey would have been impossible. Many churches have labyrinths which congregants can use as a spiritual tool to connect with Source for wisdom, guidance, and spiritual grace. Walking a labyrinth can bring openness, clarity and a sense of peace. Walking a labyrinth can be a powerful meditative tool for tapping into the wonder and mystery of life.

As a way of harvesting your life, perhaps you will choose to record your story in order to write an autobiography to share with your family. Or maybe you will choose not to do any of these but merely to remember and to reflect on questions like Brandon Burchard poses: "Did I Live, Did I love, Did I Matter?" "What did I come here to learn?" "What did I come here to teach?" Questions like these give depth and meaning to the human experience. If you choose to go deeper into self- exploration, the following questions may be useful: "How well did I live, not where did I live?" Did I live life to the hilt? Did I choose life or death every day? Who did I love and how well did I love? How well was I /am I loved? When did I fail in my desire to show love? Did I matter? Of what accomplishment am I most proud?

How have I contributed to the greater good of my family, community, state, country?

As answers to these questions come to mind, many adventures will be remembered.

In the search to know who we are, the study of ancestry has become very popular and amazing facts and stories are being unearthed. In thinking about my family and my ancestry I realized that a fore bearer had fought in every war since the Revolutionary War. It is interesting to ponder how the history of my family has been affected by the history of the country. My Great Grand Father was the first whose experiences have been passed down in our family, (see below.)My Mother's brothers were foot soldiers in World War I, my husband and his brother were drafted into WW II. My boy friends and classmates fought in Korea and my brothers were in Viet Nam. My brother who was a Marine died mysteriously at age 38, and was declared a victim of Agent Orange 30 years later. The long red line of history and war has been very prevalent in the history of my family.

One of the most treasured items in our extended family is a collection of letters written by my Great Grand Father as he fought on the Southern side in the Civil War. He was a Vermont Yankee who had graduated from Dartmouth, come South and married, then fought on the Southern side during the Civil War. He was wounded at the battle of Gettysburg, died in prison at Point Lookout, Maryland, and is buried in the family plot in St. Johnsbury, Vermont. This shared heritage of his poignant letters has been a binding cohesive force in the extended family of my cousins and their children.

One of my favorite stories from a time of war is about oatmeal cookies. A time of great anxiety for a family is having a loved one on the front lines in a war, as my

Marine brother was in the jungles of Viet Nam. Every time the phone rang my heart would stand still until I was assured that the call was not a report of his injury or death.

About that time the United States government came under heavy criticism not only for the war but for spending millions of dollars to warehouse government supported surplus food. So a program was started to distribute it to the needy. My once-a-week maid was eligible and would bring home five pound boxes of oatmeal. Since she could in no way eat that much oatmeal, she gave some of it to me and I made oatmeal cookies by the hundreds and sent them to Viet Nam. My brother never mentioned the oatmeal cookies and I have no idea if he received them, or if they had molded and he threw them away. But I had visions of the jungle trails of Viet Nam being littered with my oatmeal cookies. I hope some of the Vietnamese children were nourished by them.

Taking a trip down memory lane may be the most useful way for to remember significant events. Remembering where you were "when" is a good way to start. I was a little girl at the Monday matinee at one of our two movie theatres, which we called picture shows, when the announcement was made that President Roosevelt had died. President Franklin Roosevelt is one of our family's heroes because he had turned Warm Springs, GA. into a rehabilitation center for people disabled by polio and a member of my family was the beneficiary of those services when she was a child. Where were you when JFK was killed or when the twin towers were hit? "We all have a story to tell."

A fun way to tell your story is as though you are telling a fairy tale. You may want to make a game of it with the children in your life. After all, every good story begins, "Once Upon a Time." The exercise below was adapted from Jean Houston's *"Sing in the Muse"* exercise.

Once upon A Time, there was a_____, who lived in_____, lived with_____, who liked __ _____, who played_____, who worried about_____, who was afraid of_____, who went to_____, who decided to_____, who worked _____who worked with_____, who accomplished_____, who is proud of_____, who learned_____ who is worried about____, who fears_____, who struggles_____, who traveled where? Saw what___? Who taught? _____, suffered? ___, attempted?_____ lost? _____ Strived to? _____ and now yearns for?

The questions and musings I have included are simply a guide for you. What is the first thing that pops into your mind when I ask you about your life? What was your happiest time? What was the saddest time? What are you still mad about? What or who did you forgive? Who or what have been your most significant teachers? What have been the guiding values of your life? What do you want your legacy to be? The many different stages of life require us to play many different roles. What are the roles you have played as a daughter or son, wife/mother, husband/father, worker, community leader, activist? What are the gifts of each stage? What are the gifts to each stage?

What do you feel has been your major accomplishment? What one thing do you want your children to remember about you? What do you want your legacy to be? And what else…and what else? As you pass on your stories, and your wisdom to the next generation you can shape their lives.

We can reframe our life story by looking at the whole journey and realize that our struggles and difficulties have made us who we are and have brought us to this place. As we think of the questions, "What did I come here to learn and what did I come here to teach?" we can also ponder what our life calling has been. Perhaps your life calling has been to serve or to pray, to parent or to provide.

As we look at the whole cloth of our life we will uncover many forgotten deeds of kindness, many beautiful friendships, many unexpected acts of love and compassion that were gifts to us and that we gave to others. They are calls for celebration.

A song I like to sing at birthday celebrations has the following words; "We celebrate your being here as a gift of God to History."

Each of us is a gift of God to history and as we live out of that knowledge we can renew and reclaim those gifts for the benefit of future generations.

A movie called *The Five people You Meet in Heaven* is a wonderful example of a re-framed story. An ordinary man has lived his life as a maintenance man for a circus, he feels defeated by life because he has not been able to make his dreams of success come true. He feels his life has been worthless and he dies a depressed, hopeless man. However, when he gets to Heaven he meets the five people who were the major players in his life drama and he sees his life as beautiful and fulfilled.

Antonio Machado sums up best in this excerpt from his poem, *Last Night As I Was Sleeping.*

> *Last night as I was sleeping*
> *I dreamt—marvelous error!*
> *-that I had a beehive*
> *here inside my heart*
> *And the golden bees*
> *were making white combs*
> *and sweet honey*
> *from my old failures.*

Go Deeper

To have a great celebration of your life we need to pull out all the stops. We need to open all our boxes, our boxes of candy, of fireworks, of cake mix, our tool box, our paint box, our jewelry box. We should all dress in our red clothes, after all red is the color of celebration, of Valentine's Day, of Christmas, even Chinese New Year. Red poppies are worn on Memorial Day, and red hearts remind us of Valentine's Day and true love. Red is the power color, the color of blood, the life force.

o What is the story or fairy tales that has shaped your life?

o What do you want your family to remember about you?

o When have you faced your fear and conquered it?

o What accomplishment are you most proud of?

○ What do you want your legacy to be?

Going Lightly

○ Put on your best red clothes and do a Happy Dance, Dance as though no one is watching.

○ Celebrate your life by shouting "Yes, Yes, Yes."

○ Open a bottle of Champagne and celebrate your one unrepeatable life.

Lake and Maple

I want to give myself
utterly
as this maple
that burned and burned
for three days without stinting
and then in two more
dropped off every leaf;
as this late that,
no matter what comes
to its green-blue depths,
both takes and returns it.
in the still heart,
that refuses nothing,
the world is twice-born---
two earths wheeling,
two heavens,
two egrets reaching
down into subtraction.

Jane Hirshfield

CHAPTER ELEVEN

GIVE BACK

From what we get, we can make a living, what we give, however, makes a life. Arthur Ashe

In present culture we use the term, pay it forward, which was made popular by the movie of the same name. A young teen ager has a social studies assignment to think of and implement an idea that can improve mankind. His idea is to do three good deeds to unsuspecting recipients and ask them not to pay it back, but pay it forward, so that the random acts of kindness can multiply to change the world, thus the story unfolds.

Our human instincts tell us that we should be only concerned for ourselves, our needs, our wants. The trouble with this attitude is we never have enough. We want more and more and more. We want a bigger house, fancier food, fancier clothes. In Maslow's hierarchy of needs when the basic needs for food, clothing, shelter, safety are met, we can move into higher fulfillment of needs. The problem comes in that ego gratification beyond the basic levels cry out more and more. If we have a home, we want a larger house, then a Mansion, then a vacation house or two. There is no end when insatiable ego needs drive us and ease and pleasure are the motivation. Society has told us that we need to strive to get more and more in order to be "happy."

We admire competitive people who strive to control and dominate. In this time of hedonism we are held captive by the love of money and the things that money can buy. But in reality, money is only a medium of exchange that was invented about 4,500 years ago. Money is a symbol of our blood, sweat and tears, and is energy made visible.

If we have lived to the age of retirement we have been the beneficiary of many people's sacrifices and struggles. Occasionally someone will post in a letter to the editor a complaint about paying school taxes after their children are grown. My husband is appalled that someone could be so short sighted and responds, "Don't they know this is the price of a civil society?" We are paying it forward for at least one more generation.

Pope Francis calls money the new 'Golden Calf.' It is true that poor people worry about money, but rich people do too and the worry is the same, "Is there going to be enough?"

Charles Darwin believed that 'survival of the fittest' was the basic premise that had powered evolution as species, human and animal, competed with each other for food, water and habitat. However, recently evolutionary scientists have come to believe that cooperation was the key to survival. New evidence concludes that because humans banded together and cooperated to forage and hunt, to ward off enemies, and to protect their young, they were able to survive the harsh conditions of primitive life. Competition is still a major motivator but few will deny that cooperation is necessary in every aspect of life.

In our present society are "givers"," takers," "matchers" and "users." We know people who have a generosity of spirit; they are community and church volunteers. They are the 20% who do the grunt work of any organization, serving on the Boards as well as working like a dog to man the latest charity event. They find great joy in donating, time, talent or money to any cause they are passionate about.

The "takers" live only for themselves and would not "give you the time of day." These people possibly live with their fists closed so nothing can flow in, and nothing can flow out. The "matchers" will give, but only if they get equal or more value in return. They become a member only if the organization gives tickets or free dinners or T- shirts as part of the membership. Then there are people who are "users", they use friendship, memberships, and contacts to further their own purposes. I live in an area of the country where there is a poverty mentality as opposed to an abundance mentality. While people in my area of the country are "givers", they are usually more generous with their time than with their money.

You might want to gauge whether you live out of a poverty mentality, an abundance mentality or a sufficiency mentality. Where in this construct do you see yourself? We probably can classify in each category according to the circumstances of the day. We are bombarded with requests to support many worthy causes. And usually we choose which to support based on our personal involvement with the need as when a family member has one of the catastrophic illnesses.

Other times we respond to a natural disaster somewhere in the world because the need is so great and the devastation so severe. Many times a service organization has chosen a certain focus as their primary charity, such as Shriners and their work with children's medical needs. We also remember the Lion's Clubs and their work with the blind and donation of eyeglasses. Meanwhile, the local not for profit organizations depend on local people to help meet the needs in their community.

When I was first introduced to the United Nations Millennium Development Goals, I was stunned. How could any organization, even the U.N. hope to substantially reduce poverty, illiteracy, infant mortality in a brief 10 year period. My friend, Anele Heiges, a

Dominican nun, works at the UN to raise world- wide awareness of the sexual trafficking of women and children. So I asked Anele how it would be possible for the UN to reach such impossible goals in such a short time. Who was going to make this happen? Her answer, "There are Legions of Angels, there are legions of angels" was stunning and her answer caused me to think for years.

Then I went to a seminar at Florida State University, sponsored by the Art Therapy Department, and heard a woman architect from California tell about her life work. She teaches women in South East Asia to recover the lost art of harvesting silk thread, then dyeing the silk and weaving traditional patterns, which she uses in design work for her upper echelon clients. The recovery of this ancient skill afforded the women a livelihood for their families and an education for their children. For the first time I felt I was in the presence of one of those Legions of Angels.

Another member of the Legion of Angels is a man named Mohammed Yunnus who established Grameen Bank in Bangladesh to provide microcredit to the poorest of the poor. In 31 years he has loaned 2.5 billion dollars to mostly women with a 98% repayment rate. When he received the Noble Peace Prize, the presenters noted that lasting peace cannot be achieved unless ways are found to help people break out of poverty. Dr. Yunnus believes that Bangladesh will achieve the Millennium Development Goals by 2015 and will eradicate poverty completely by the year 2050. Amazing.

Who do you know that are unsung members of the Legion of Angels? We admire Bill Gates, Warren Buffet, Jimmy Carter and others who use their wealth and influence to make a difference. People who have earned or inherited great wealth many times feel a responsibility to make a contribution to the good of the world. Warren Buffet had challenged billionaires to give away most of their wealth by the time of their death and many have responded. Bill Gates has led the way as he has used the wealth of his foundation to eradicate many of the preventable illnesses in the developing world. Jimmy Carter is widely known for his support of Habitat for Humanity and international work on behalf of peace. What a contrast between these men and the robber barons who led the industrial revolution in this country.

Over the next 50 years an estimated $40-plus trillion dollars will pass from one generation to the next in the United States. This historic transfer of wealth presents an opportunity to change the face of philanthropic giving from gifts from immensely wealthy donors to gifts from ordinary people who have a vision of how their money could be used to impact the world, their community, or their favorite charity.

Scientists are proposing that we have come to the end of our physical evolution as a species and that our challenge is to create a cultural evolution. We have been reminded that a society is judged by the way it treats its most deprived and helpless. As we look at our world with its hatred, divisions, hunger, and wars we have no doubt about the way we will be judged. We are aware that all the systems of our country are in a state of collapses.

The health care system, the political system, the education system, social service system and others that were designed to serve the common good have in many cases become not only ineffective but cruel. If we are in a time of whole systems transition, how do you think our culture needs to evolve? Where do we to start? How do we evolve as individuals? How do we become new people able to meet the challenges of this age?

Native Americans tell us that we should make every decision by the standard of how it will affect seven generations from our own. It is hard to imagine how my decisions can affect Caroline, my great grand-daughter's, great grand-children. My only hope is that by living more sustainably I can help to pass on to her an earth that is fit for human habitation.

What does the world need that you can give that will make a difference for future generations?

Paul Hawken, in his book, "Blessed Unrest", cites that there are two million voluntary non- profit organizations that are working to create a world that works for everyone. Assuming that each organization has 20 committed volunteers who bring in at least 100 more to work on special projects, that is a lot of people. I am not good at math, so you do it. With that many people at work for good causes, why is not a larger impact being felt? What else is needed? While we are social activist to the max, Andrew Harvey challenges us to combine our social activism with a new depth of openness and commitment to love and become spiritual activists.

The times demand that we become more, with deeper spirits, understanding, more open to change, more open to new possibilities, more compassionate, more loving, more centered. But how? We have been unconscious for too long, our focus has been diverted by mass media telling the story they want us to not only hear but believe: materialism is good, war is inevitable, unlimited growth is excellent. Fear based news and mind-less entertainment have diverted our intelligence and our creativity. Our activism must be steeped in the spiritual truths that are part of every religion.

The Civil Rights Movement was the example in our time of a cause based in justice, faith and spirit. The leaders were spiritual activists grounded in teaching from the Old and New Testament and were willing to suffer and die to change one of the cruelty systems. Who could ever forget the courage of the young man standing in front of the tank in Tiananmen Square in protest when the movement toward democracy in China was brutally crushed? Many other spiritual activists face death for the cause of freedom and justice. We honor environmental heroes like Tim DeChristopher who went to jail to protest the auction of oil and gas leases on federal lands in Utah and is now enrolled in Divinity School at Harvard.

Albert Einstein said that "problems cannot be solved with the same mind-set that created them." He also said that our task must be to widen our circle of compassion to embrace all living creatures and the whole of nature in beauty.

Is the question of the times, 'How do we create or harvest the new mind-set that is needed to shift the problems that have escalated since the beginning of the industrial age"? How do we become spiritual activists, with every decision based on its impact on the 7th generation and the good of the world? Spirituality and activism can no longer be separated. The time of becoming a wandering ascetic or a monk is gone, but discipline and commitment are still required. Retreats, pilgrimages, meditation, poetry, disciplines of prayer and study are fuel for the hard task of taking our convictions for a more just, sustainable world to the streets and becoming spiritual activists. What is the new world waiting to be called forth? Is it the Beloved Community that Martin Luther King, Jr. spoke of?

People are exploring new expressions of the longing for deeper connection with the Divine. These may be part of many traditional practices, churches, temples, synagogues or they may be ad hoc and not related to any formal structure. On-line courses are being offered by well- known spiritual teachers in which thousands of people participate and become part of virtual communities devoted to conscious evolution, prayer, mysticism, Christ consciousness or integral spirituality and on and on. These are just the ones I know about. When a Southern Baptist preacher's daughter becomes a Buddhist nun and lives at Plum Village, we know we are not in the Kansas anymore. On the other hand, mega churches draw thousands of worshippers to be inspired and entertained by a charismatic leader. How do we combine social activism with spiritual activism?

The winds of change are blowing.

We can become more conscious of the task before us and how our talents and interests and commitment can contribute. We can determine to grow deeper, to be more in tune with the Soul's call. We can cross religious and cultural boundaries to embrace practices of prayer and worship from many traditions like ton glen from the Buddhist tradition or the Corn Dance of the Navajo people. We can show appreciation for Mother Earth in all her glory by caring for her and singing love songs to her. Our participation in whole systems transition requires that we bring the best of our intellectual faculties and our spiritual commitment to bear on the issues, whether they are the monetary system, the prison system, the welfare system, the health care system, and others.

I invite you to join the Legions of Angels who will

create new possibilities. We may not be able to impact a whole country but we never know how our influence will be used for good. "It is a terrible thing to fall into the hands of the Living God," to step into the highest form of service. How can we give of ourselves, of our essence, out of a sense of compassion for the other's journey? It takes courage and commitment to answer the call and perseverance to see the journey to the end. The "flying monkeys" of self-doubt and the "wart hogs" of your fears will try to stop you. They will be "yapping at your heels, turn back, turn back." This heroic journey requires competence, stamina, pizazz and a sense of humor.

Times are demanding that we give back in expression of our gratitude to those who have gone before, but even more to build a future for the generations to come and that we find new ways of giving back by paying it forward.

Around 1960, the women of the Colquitt Methodist Church sent some money to Hong Kong to buy school supplies for refugee children after the Communist take-over of Mainland China. Somehow my name was on one of the boxes, and I received a letter of thanks from a Mr. C.S. Chow. It was written by his daughter, Christine, on her father's behalf since he did not speak English. They were so appreciative and later sent me some small plastic replicas of US Presidents from the plastics factory where he worked. He had been an important government official in the Chaing Kai-shek regime, and they had been wealthy. He had fled to Hong Kong with his wife and seven children and an amah, and another child was born after their escape. We exchanged letters and I sent them Christmas cards with pictures of my family. I asked what they would like to have that I could send them. More than anything the family wanted a radio, so I sent $35 to purchase a radio in Hong Kong since they were manufactured there. They were most appreciative and thanked me profusely. After my third child was born and I returned to college and eventually to work, our contacts stopped. More than 25 years went by.

Then about 1990, I received a call from the Lutheran Church in a neighboring town. The Chow family was trying to find me (but I had never moved) and in just a matter of minutes, I was talking to the extended family in Hong Kong. Mr. Chow had died; they had retrieved my letters from his belongings and wanted to thank me for the radio, again.

In 1994, Christine came to the US to visit her daughter, Emma, who was in College in Minnesota, and they spent Christmas with us in Colquitt. Then in 1995, I went on a trip to China, and the last leg was spent in Hong Kong where Christine had a full itinerary set up for me. I was met by the Red Cross (who had delivered the school supplies to the children so many years before) and an interview appeared in the local newspaper about the friendship across the generations and across the world.

The first night Mrs. Chow had a command performance dinner at a fancy restaurant to which all of her children were required to attend. The family was still thanking me for the radio which was their entertainment as children in their small world as refugees. I personally think the radio was the adults' contact with the outside world as they listened to the news from their homeland.

The next night, Mrs. Chow herself cooked a dinner of prawns for me in her small flat. Since I am about collecting stories, I kept pressing her to tell about her escape from China and her life in Hong Kong. She refused to talk about it to me or her children. After the dinner she presented me with a beautiful jacket of Chinese silk that she had sewn herself for me. Then she gave me the most beautiful bracelet I have ever seen. It is 10 carat gold set with Russian diamonds and pearls from her dowry. I nearly fainted.

Why would she give me something so valuable, when she was far from wealthy? Her reply stunned me when she said, "We lived in the card board shacks in the hills above the City, and life was so hard I would think I could not go on. Then I would remember that there was someone halfway around the world who cared and I would take courage."

While you wipe away your tears, I will tell you to hang on, that is not all the story. In April 1998, a Hong Kong television station sent a film crew to Colquitt to do a story on the friendship across the years. They sent a producer and a cameraman to Colquitt, a town of 2,000, to do a segment of their series denoting friendships across the world. During the week-end of our local Mayhaw festival, the crew was busy filming local people, the Mayhaw festival parade and the Swamp Gravy performance.

When the segment was shown in Hong Kong, the culture of the south was shown in all its small town glory. As the Swamp Gravy cast sang "Amazing Grace", lit memorial candles and called out "C.S. Chow, 'I Remember You'", a picture of Mr. Chow as it appears on his tombstone was shown. Across the globe, two cultures, two time periods, two families were linked because one very small random act of kindness had such a long history and impacted several generations. What a life: "You can't make this stuff up."

Go Deeper

Green is the color of money and also the color of the foliage of the natural world. The green trees allow us to breathe as they give out oxygen and take in the carbon dioxide that is polluting our atmosphere. This is the perfect example of the symbiotic relationship that humans have had for eons with Nature.

○ From your paint box take out your many shades of green colors.

○ We have three things to give or to give back or to pay forward: our time, our resources of money, or our talents which all together adds up to ourselves.

○ On a scale of one to ten rate yourself as a giver, a taker, a matcher or a user. Use the different colors of green to denote your scores. Be as objective as you can.

○ How do you choose where to make your gifts of time money or talent?

○ What is the pay back for you? Is it recognition for your donation or a feeling of generosity?

○ Do you give a tithe of 10% of your income as a way of saying thank you.

○ What cause would you die for?

Go Lightly

○ Do something for yourself that fills you with happiness and hope. Singing in the church choir does it for me.

○ Do something for an acquaintance, relative or stranger that is completely unexpected.

○ Plant a tree or a forest and help green the world.

○ 'Give it up' is a term used to denote applause as a way of showing appreciation. Think of a way to 'give it up' for a job well done.

○ Pay it forward in myriad ways: by buying a meal for the person in line behind you.

○ Choose one way each day to green the world.

JOY

Joy is an old-fashioned word.
What did it used to mean?

Like "happy" maybe?
Or was it "silly" and "giggly?"
Could just anyone get to it?
Or was it buried in book and brow?

I wish I knew
What it used to mean,
For I need a word,
A good, solid word.

That shows how I feel
When the day is over
And I've worked well
And I'm glad to be so tired.

I need a word for when

I've spent hours and hours
With those I love, and I'm
Talk-sore and smile-aching.

I need a word for when
I'm alone, and over the miles
Are parts of my heart, deep in others
Who are warm, and safe, and at peace.

I need a word for when
A job looms like a greyhound
And I can do it, and I want to do it
And I tingle to get at it.

I need a word for that
Warm, gentle flow that
Covers every corner of my being.
And says, "Lo I am with you always."

I need a word
Real bad,
And I think it might be

"joy"

Or maybe it's
"God."
Then again, maybe
They're the same
Word.

        Unknown

CHAPTER TWELVE

SPREAD JOY

More and More

"Joy is a net of love,

by which to catch souls." Mother Teresa

The memory that fills me with the most joy happened on November 22, 1996, the night that the Swamp Gravy cast performed at the Kennedy Center in Washington, D.C. The beginning of Swamp Gravy had been rocky; we had performed a one hour show based on our community's stories in October of 1992. We did not mount a show in 1993 because our funds from donations and a Georgia Humanities grant were spent. But through perseverance and hard work we were able to present our first full two hour show in 1994. Unbelievably, two years later, we were invited to take Swamp Gravy to the Kennedy Center. When I stood in the audience at the Kennedy Center and watched the teacher, shopkeepers, housewives and children of our little town tell the stories of their heritage, I thought I would burst with pride and joy.

When have you felt unbridled "joy"? Was it when you first looked into the face of your newborn child? When was the last time you experienced joy, -beyond pleasure, beyond happiness, beyond satisfaction? What was the occasion? How did you feel?

"Why all this embarrassment About being happy? Sometimes I'm as happy as a sleeping dog and for the same reasons, And for others." Wendell Berry

During the holiday season the word "Joy" appears on greeting cards, wrapping paper, ornaments, as we are constantly reminded of the world joy. What does it mean? What is the message that is being transmitted to us, consciously or subliminally?

To be joyful is to be dynamically alive at any age. Feelings of happiness and well-being flood our body with endorphins that invigorate our mind and renew our body. Bruce Lipton calls this the honeymoon effect. When we are in love every moment is full of excitement, anticipation and good will for everyone and everything, This state of mind and heart is to be sought, envied, and enjoyed.

Abraham Lincoln attested to the fact that we are as happy as we make up our minds to be. Mike Dooly says in his, *Notes from the Universe*, that "everyone has a built-in happiness button which can instantly change how they feel, but for many, most of the time they prefer not to push it."

Is joy an innate gift we are born with or is it the result of reconciling life's problems and sorrows and arriving at a place of peace? Is joy a beginning place or an end? Babies seem to have an in born sense of joy; they love smiling, playing peek-a-boo, laughing out loud and do not develop normally without this playful interaction with others.

My name is Joy, so all of my life when I had reason to be sad or disgruntled or angry I would remember that I am supposed to be the embodiment of "joy" and change my attitude. I did not have a happy nurturing childhood but by tapping into a place that could not be touched by circumstances, I was able to keep my spirit intact and not live out of my wounded child.

We Americans look for more and more material possessions to fill us with contentment, and we have not yet learned that happiness is not a by- product of things. We suffer from Abundanza, the affliction of too muchness and we are burdened down by our prosperity, which includes larger houses, more closets, more stuff, and more money. We worry and fret and spend entirely too much energy and money protecting, cleaning and multiplying our myriad possessions.

In contrast, Calcutta, India, has been named the City of Joy. It is one of the poorest cities in the world where millions live in abject poverty, disease and filth, but laughter and good humor fill the streets. On seeing the stage play entitled "Calcutta" Mother Teresa told the cast that they were giving joy by their actions while her nuns were doing the same by their service. What a beautiful example of honoring two very different ways of bringing joy. (from Everything Starts with Prayer by Mother Teresa)

Robbers of our joy are all around us. Everything goes

wrong first thing on some morning, setting the tone for the day. Do you remember the cartoon showing how the bad mood of a boss goes down the pecking order to the father, then the wife, then the child, until the family dog gets kicked at the end of the day?

We allow negativity and judgment of people to dominate our thinking and we take on the struggles of friends and family and make them our own. We are harried, stressed, worried as we wallow in self- pity and feel used, treated unfairly, unlucky. We feel we are losing control of our lives and blame ourselves, even as we blame and judge others. The popular term for this state is "sweating the small stuff." The troubles and care of life separate us from a sense of peace and contentment which is the basis of joy. We wallow in gossip and self-pity, and recite "ain't it awful stories." Why is this happening to me?"

The Holiday Season brings out all these raw emotions. When my children were young, I was a working mother, and I remember the feelings of "how am I going to get it all done, where does each child have to be at what time and with what gifts? I was not in the Christmas spirit and was expressing verbally my feeling of stress. An older friend of mine taught me a valuable lesson when she said that with every gift she wraps she remembers with joy and gratitude how much she loves that person. Frances died in her forties with a congenital heart condition, and I remember her words of wisdom every Christmas season.

Each of us handles our own problems as well as other people's hardships in different ways. Hyper-sensitive people take on other people's worries and sorrows, and their health is affected. As a child my cousin would cry all night with her legs hurting after visiting a friend who was incapacitated by polio. Some people can be sympathetic, empathetic, and helpful without being caught in a place of the empath. Some people can share the burdens of neighbors or relatives in wholesome, helpful ways, doing what they can but not letting others problems sink them into a personal depression or crisis of faith. The psychological pull of the news media recounting countless horror stories is harmful to our emotional health.

We need disciplines that help us overcome this such as prayer for victims of tragedy, gifts of money, friendship, support in times of death and illness, and don't forget the Southern way of bringing comfort food in times of grief. A group of my friends spent many weeks in Newtown, CT, helping the victims recover by doing a process called Emotional Freedom Technique, which involves tapping on the meridians of the body thus releasing the pain and trauma. This method, commonly called tapping, has become a widely used therapy for healing.

Downward spirals of depression start with unawareness of what brings us joy. Thoughtless words and actions from friends, bosses or acquaintances can leave us devastated. People and situations we encounter seem intent on stealing our joy, and real problems of illness, addiction and death cannot be handled glibly. One of my greatest learnings is to take nothing personally since most of the time, it is not about you, personally or professionally, but comes from the emotional issues projected on you by your nemesis.

Probably, my most painful experience was the time my very best friend betrayed my trust during an important project that we were partnering to create. Plus, I lost another dear friend in the drama that ensued. I was so hurt that I wanted to die and actually felt that I had a hole where my heart should have been. My heartache was a visceral experience as well as an emotional one. Fortunately a massage therapist friend used energy techniques to heal the hole in my heart, and I could go forward with my plans. I learned from this event, namely, that there is life after deep emotional pain and scarring. I learned to forgive but also how hard forgiveness is. I wish I could report that my joy was intact during this time, but it was not. I suffered terribly, and my joy did not return until the project came to a beautiful fulfillment.

What makes you feel full of joy? Is it the singing of children? Is it the hugs of grandchildren? Is it the light in children's eyes when they see Santa Claus? Is it when you feel that you are loved by a special person? Do we forget how to be joyful and joy filled?

I propose that one of the easiest ways to become joyful is to become filled with beauty. Emily Dickinson writes in one of her poems,

Inebriate of air am I,
And debauchee of dew,
Reeling through endless summer days,
From inns of molten blue."

Finding joy is about waking up and experiencing the beauty which is everywhere. Flowers remind us of happy experiences. In the midst of the Southern winter, the delicate beauty of the camellia blossoms lifts my mood out of the winter doldrums. The narcissus blossoms, white as snow, perfume the air and perfume our spirits. Of the six children in our family, five of us were born in early spring, so my Mother always said that when she looked out her bedroom window and saw the daffodils blooming she thought she should have a new baby. When we enjoy the beauty of flowers we are reminded of the wonders of creation and the Mystery of the Creator.

Music, for me, is another way to enter the state of

consciousness called joy. One of my greatest experiences of unbounded joy happened while lying on a quilt in a field and pretending that the stars were an orchestra that I was conducting while Beethoven's Fifth Symphony was booming its majesty. Imagine, Baabaaboom, baabaaboom. Tadada,tadada, tadada, tadada, tadadadoom. The sublime beauty of the night sky and Beethoven's music filled me with ecstasy.

I, also, had an experience during the Holiday season like James Wright describes when he said that "Suddenly I realized that if I stepped out of my body I would break into blossom." I was singing in a Christmas cantata at my local church and at the end of the Hallelujah Chorus, I unexpectedly raised my arms and let out a most unsophisticated "Wow." It was the most spontaneous act of natural joy that I have ever expressed. I am still amused, amazed and a little embarrassed at my exuberance.

Christians sing "Joy to the World" while children and young at hearts sing:

"Jeremiah was a bullfrog. He was a good friend of mine. Singing-Joy to the World, all the boys and girls, Joy to the fishes in the deep blue sea, and Joy to you and me."

Many of Nature's gifts touch a deep cord and send subliminal messages to our Spirits through their symbolic presence. For instance, rainbows remind us of the promises of God as spelled out in the Old Testament. Butterflies speak to us of transformation as the ugly worm in the cocoon becomes a beautiful flying flower. Bluebirds are the symbol of comfort and hope for my sister and me, and to friends seeing a lady bug brings good luck. Sunrises and sunsets bring poignant memories of times gone by and times yet to come. We are blessed by the unconditional love of pets and the fun they bring into our lives.

Small acts of kindness can bring back our joy and bring solace to others when life gets hard. Thoughtful deeds, such as a card or phone call, a hug or a handshake, makes our hearts expand. Sincere compliments also can cause a lifting of the spirit and bring happiness. Akin to paying a compliment is the act of giving encouragement. Compliments speak to past acts while encouragement boosts morale and paves the way for the future. The generosity of the open heart looks for ways to share love, laughter and joy. The hospitality of the open home or the open heart shares warmth and joy.

There are many examples of people who spread joy such as Jarrett Mynear, a young boy, who started the Joy cart to deliver toys to sick children in the Kentucky Children's hospital where he was a patient and eventually died of cancer. Flash Mobs appear in surprising venues such as train stations, international airports to spread joy to unsuspecting bystanders. My favorite way to spread joy is by sharing free hugs and it is also my favorite way to have fun. Joy, like gratitude, is a spring that eternally refills as you give it away.

As we mature we realize that Joy comes from the soul level and is reclaimed through practices of forgiveness, reconciliation, and acceptance of the journey of our lives. As this journey unfolds before us, as loved ones die and new generations are born, we experience the unfolding saga of the long red line of humanity. Friends move or fade from our lives, and new friends enrich us in unexpected ways.

Joseph Campbell introduced the idea of walking the Pollen Path as a way to experience joy. Navajo legend from which the pollen path is taken, names it the Path of Beauty and Path to the Center. The image of the pollen path is different for everyone, but my image of it is walking down a path that is lined with amazingly beautiful flowers that are giving their life force, their regenerative power to the wind and all who pass by. The pollen path, to me, I call living in the flow, bring open to the nudges and opportunities that create the miraculous. Those who live on the Pollen Path carry a spirit of beauty, creativity, life giving energy and joy with them and give it without regard for circumstances or situation.

This Christmas I had an experience of being in the flow. On Christmas Eve I went to my church to give a Christmas gift to Rebecca, my minister. When I entered the back hall, I heard children's voices and followed them. Our church custodian, Mary, and her grandchildren were coming to meet me. I asked the children if they were excited that Santa Claus was coming, and the girl responded, "There ain't no Santa Claus." I was taken aback by the hardness of her tone.

She was past the age where she would still believe in Santa Claus, and she repeated there is no Santa Claus. I made murmurs that Santa Claus is the spirit of love and quickly made my way to find my minister.

As I was talking to her, Mary interrupted us to say that her granddaughter and grandson were not getting any Christmas presents because their Mother was out of work and she had no money for gifts. Rebecca's face was totally stricken as I am sure mine was too. When I got home I called Mary and was able to give her some money for the children. Tears were running down her face when I pressed the money in her hand. I tell this story not for accolades for myself, but to demonstrate the way being in the flow works. If I had not gone to the church, if Mary's grandchildren had not been with her, if I had not spoken to the children, if Mary had not shared their plight, If, If, If. But it all happened as if there was a design and those children did not have the heart break of no gifts on Christmas Day.

As we spread joy, our hearts are full of gratitude for every gift of life.

Go Deeper

What do you think of when you think of the word 'Joy?' *I think of champagne.* It is quiet and contained when it is under pressure. When it is opened it bubbles up and fizzes out of the bottle. The iridescent bubbles remind us to float full of life and color. Joy is like champagne, it is a calm quiet essence most of the time, but when it is released it bubbles up and fills the room with laughter. Joy bubbles up inside you when you least expect it.

○ What makes you full of joy? Is it hugs from special people? Is it a calm knowledge that all is well no matter the outer circumstances to the contrary?

○ Do we forget to be joyful and joy filled? How can you bring more joy into your life?

○ Think of a person who brings joy to others? Do they work quietly behind the scenes on a daily basis? Or are they a 'larger than life' person who walks the pollen path and spreads joy by their presence.

Go Lightly

In your toy box I hope you have a wand used to blow bubbles. I like the big wands that make bubbles the size of dinner plates.

○ Make a soapy solution by mixing dish detergent with water.

o Go outside and blow bubbles, if possible with a child and take note of the different colors reflected in the bubbles

o Take a bubble bath and luxuriate in experience.

o Take a walk under the full moon and sing a children's lullaby. For instance:

"I see the moon and the moon sees me

And the moon sees the one that I want to see.

God bless the moon and God bless me

And God bless the one that I want to see."

o Sing wherever you can, in the shower, in the rain, in a chorus, to a child.

o On your paper, draw iridescent bubbles and think of all the people who bring you joy.

The Place I Want
to Get Back To

The place I want to get back to

is where

in the pinewoods

in the moment between

the darkness

and first light

two deer

came walking down the hill

and when they saw me

they said to each other, okay,

this one is okay,

let's see who she is

and why she is sitting

on the ground, like that,

so quiet, as if

asleep, or in a dream,

but, anyway, harmless;

and so they came

on their slender legs

and gazed upon me

not unlike the way

I go out to the dunes and look

and look and look

into the faces of the flowers;

and then one of them leaned forward

and nuzzled my hand, and what can my life

bring to me that could exceed

that brief moment?

For twenty years

I have gone every day to the same woods,

not waiting, exactly, just lingering.

Such gifts, bestowed, can't be repeated.

If you want to talk about this

come to visit. I live in the house

near the corner, which I have named

<u>Gratitude</u>.

Mary Oliver

CHAPTER THIRTEEN

EXPRESS GRATITUDE

"Every Day A Holiday,

Every Meal A Feast." Billy Kimbrel

It is fitting that the final chapter in this challenge to age dynamically be named gratitude. Many different expressions mean gratitude; i.e. appreciation, gratefulness, thankfulness and are used interchangeably. Brother David Stendl-Rast is a Benedictine monk whose life-work is expressing gratitude and inviting others to live a life enmeshed in the art of gratitude. He has made the practice of gratefulness a part of popular culture through his books, web-site and his appearances at religious and secular conferences. He crosses the boundaries of all religious traditions, acknowledging and affirming that we are all One with different ways of approaching the God Head. The uniting ritual of all faiths is gratefulness as he perceives it. What is gratitude? Is gratitude a once in a while feeling or a habit, a way of life, or an attitude of mind and heart?

Notice the play on words Great Attitude. A great attitude is the basis of gratitude. Another play on words the "great fullness" has been made popular by Brother David. The words "great fullness" bring the words out of the head and into the body. Do you feel the great fullness in your body?

A conference called the Poetry of Gratefulness features Bro. David Stendl-Rast. On the YouTube renderings of the conference, you can watch Lynn Twist talk about the difference between gratefulness and thanksgiving as she learned it from Bro. David Stendl-Rast. With great joy she talks about gratefulness as the "great full ness" that overflows into thanksgiving. When you are thankful all you want to do is share and make a difference and when you share and make a difference it overflows into gratefulness. So it is a self-replenishing fountain that is never empty. Such a fountain fills us with adventure and aliveness and love for all creatures. Lynne demonstrates, in her incomparable way, that gratefulness and thanksgiving are different sides of the same coin.

When we think of gratitude it is a no-brainer. If we are the least bit awake, of course, we are grateful for the gift of life, for family, for our journey. When we see a beautiful sunset or we are in the presence of a special loved one, we feel grateful whether we acknowledge it or not. How about all the other times when we are ill or tragedy strikes? Gratitude in the midst of these experiences is a different story. We are so caught up in the pain of the experience that gratitude is the farthest thing from our mind and we cannot possibly be thankful at moments like this. It takes the heart of a mystic to be grateful for every experience of life, beautiful or unpleasant. Even as we grow older, we realize that our life experiences have made us who we are and taught us the life lessons that made us grow. Still it is hard to be grateful for the pain, loss and mistakes that have made detours on our path.

When does the sheer beauty and magnificence of the world fill you with gratitude? My favorite place to experience profound gratitude is on a beautiful beach, looking at the endless expanse of water. For some people the mountains, filled with grandeur, remind them to be thankful. Such occasions remind us of our smallness and helplessness and fill us with awe.

Many occasions for gratitude present themselves: such

as a special unexpected gift, a hand written card expressing love and admiration. I am most grateful for a new friend who came into my life unexpectedly and has blessed and enriched me immeasurably. Can you think of such a friend? I am grateful for meaningful ways to engage with others who are committed to the work that makes a difference in the world and that presents us with opportunities to grow.

When we have no sense of gratitude we can become critical and resentful, and beset by feelings of victimization. We live in a culture of complaining, we never have enough, we want more and more for less and less effort. We feel a sense of entitlement: we should have been born richer, more beautiful, with parents who were more loving, or a spouse who is more understanding. When we capitulate to depression we can lose our motivation.

Gratitude gives us the opportunity to reframe our past experiences, to lay down our psychic burdens and live fully in the present. Gratefulness takes us out of self-pity and shifts focus from the negative to the positive.

The field of brain research has shown that what we focus our attention on creates neural pathways in the brain. The good news is the brain's capacity to rewire itself. The more we focus on the true and good and beautiful, the more pronounced these neural connections become and we can literally re-wire our brains. We can break those connections caused by negative conditioning. We literally have the power over our own mental health. Victor Frankl said that between a stimulus and a response there is a space and in that space we have the power to choose our response. In our response is our growth and our freedom. Expressing gratitude can make us healthier, free us from emotional pain, and give us freedom from load. As we feel less pain, we make room for more happiness and joy.

The most powerful generosity is generosity of Spirit. Gratitude is a mind-set which allows us to take care of ourselves. Nancy Napier says that it is "nutritious psychological and spiritual food". Only as we love and nurture ourselves can we have eyes to see and hearts to discern the nuances of living in the spiritual plane of gratitude. The Psalms are beautiful prayers of thanksgiving and have brought comfort to countless generations. Many people pray and sing the psalms and in them find release and joy.

What are the obstacles to a daily practice of gratitude? Living a life of gratitude is not easy especially when the heart is closed to the wonder of every day.

For example, our own egocentrism. "What a good boy am I" is the underlying belief that we made it all happen. Our busyness and over involvement in "good things," caring for family, work, civic and social responsibilities is another block to gratitude as well as our emphasis on being in our head rather than our heart.

Rituals of gratitude remind us that life in more than our day to day joys and struggles. Every night, a man, who is struggling caring for his wife who has Alzheimer's disease, goes into a quiet room, turns off all the light and in the darkness, recounts the things for which he is most grateful.

The Eucharist which is a ritual celebration of the Presence of Christ is called the Great Thanksgiving. Thankfulness is the beginning of gratitude. Gratitude is the completion of thankfulness. Thankfulness may consist merely of words. Gratitude is shown in acts. Henri Frederic Amiel Facebook on Gratitude.

Gratitude is both a feeling and an expression. The most elementary expression of gratitude is saying thank you by writing a thank you note or showing appreciation to someone for a small service. Feelings of warm gratitude flood over us in the presence of friends and those who love and nurture us. Overwhelming joy and gratitude flood us when you look onto the face of a new baby and the open heart overflows in praise for life in all its beauty and complexity.

Singing has always been a favorite form of expressing heart-felt emotions. Love songs are songs of praise and appreciation for the beauty and charm of the latest lady love. Songs of gratitude and praise like the Gloria Patria, (Praise God from Whom All Blessings Flow) are sung by millions of people in houses of worship. "For the beauty of the Earth, For the Glory of the Skies, for the love which from our birth over and around us lies, Lord of all to thee we raise this hymn of grateful praise" is another well- known song of praise. The same sentiment is expressed in secular songs such as "Oh What a Beautiful Morning, Oh What a Beautiful Day" written for stage and movies. John Denver wrote beautiful ballads, such as "Morning Has Broken, like the first Morning" which speak from a grateful heart.

The Institute of Cultural affairs, in their international human development work, suggested that each community write a love song to the town where they lived. The song I sing to my town is "On the Street Where You Live." What is the love song you would like to sing to your neighborhood and community? Maybe you would compose one based on "Wonderful, Wonderful Copenhagen, and Salty old Queen of the Sea," or "New York, New York." A love song is a peon of praise to the Beloved.

Not only singing, but beautiful writing, especially poetry opens my heart with gratitude. Words that express emotions in profoundly beautiful ways stop me up short and I have to put the book down and say a silent thank you to that author for sharing heart and talent with me.

If you would like to create the inner transformation of a grateful heart, try these suggestions below:

- Nurture a generous spirit. Only when we are filled with gratitude and are in the morphic field of gratitude can we be used and tapped by God for special adventures.
- Live each day as if is the first and last days of your life, as Helen Keller suggests.
- Stand present to the wonder of your life's journey.
- Keep a gratitude journal and each day record at least 3 things that you are grateful for.
- Express out loud your appreciation to people for services or favors they have done for you; and really feel the gratitude, if it is rote, it does not count.

- Go outside your comfort zone to acknowledge your appreciation to someone you don't particularly like.
- Sing a love song to the Earth, our Mother.
- Celebrate the goodness of life. God is Good All the Time, All the Time, God is Good.

My brother Joe Sloan was 17 years younger than I; in fact, he was born when I was in college. Joe was a child of the 70's and was a product of that cultural revolution of experimentation with drugs, alcohol and sex. By the time he was 40; he had married and settled down to a job in the agricultural lending business. About that time he had an awakening experience and became a devout Christian. He became a highly respected leader in the business community and the church. He was always willing to go the extra mile to get the job done. His faith grew and his mantra became "God is Good All the Time, All the Time God is Good."

When Joe was diagnosed with lung cancer in 2009 his faith became stronger. He was not surprised; he had tried to quit smoking many times, but would always start again. When he knew he did not have long to live he asked our minister to have small crosses made inscribed with the words "God is Good, All the Time." David, our minister, was able to find a small family owned business in ME. which postponed their other orders because time was short. Joe wanted these given to the 100 people who might come to his funeral. Instead 300 crosses were given that day as we celebrated the transition of a life that in the midst of suffering believed that "God is Good All the Time."

Go Deeper

○ Please open the last box on our list, a beautiful gift box. This gift box contains the Earth, our home. The Earth from outer space is called the big blue marble, and what an amazing sight gleaming against the indigo blue sky! The pictures taken by the astronauts of the Earth from the Moon have become the new icon of our age. They remind us that Mother Earth nurtures us, gives us food and water and beauty.

The color of gratitude is blue, the blue of the infinite sky. "Blue skies smiling at me"… The feeling of blue is warmth, happiness, the feelings that are part of gratitude.

○ What activities remind you to be grateful?

○ What rituals of gratitude do you perform?

○ Is a blessing before meals part of your daily practice?

○ How do you recognize that God is Good All the Time?

Go Lightly

○ Draw a night sky full of stars and on each star write a word or symbol of something you are grateful for. You can make it a copy of Van Gogh's Starry Night.

○ Try writing a poem of thanksgiving.

○ Sing a love song to the Earth.

○ If you are so led, fly the Earth flag, which depicts the big blue marble floating on a sea of indigo blue.

○ Spend a few minutes each day looking at the clouds floating on the blue, blue sky.

○ Each time you put on a blue garment, say a prayer of gratitude.

SO WHAT?

Congratulations, you've read it to the end, or skipped around like I do, or even started at the end. Are you inspired, energized, intrigued or overwhelmed? Does reading all this make you tired? Does it seem too much? Are you ready for a time of Being and not Doing? A time to renew before you re-invent yourself?

Perhaps you will pick and choose one or two suggestions from your favorite chapter and let them percolate and take hold in your imagination. Maybe the chapter on "Pay Attention" spoke to you because you recognize that life is rushing by in a haze of "should and oughts". Or after reading the chapter on "Play", you feel the need to bring more play into your life. While you can eat an elephant one bite at a time, you can start with just a taste. Small changes lead to big results.

Some social scientists are recognizing that the years between 50 and 75, when people are neither young nor old, as a new developmental stage previously unrecognized and named. These are artificial numbers; the 50s were previously seen as mid-life, with its mid-life crises of the empty nest and a chance to renew the marriage without the focus of attention on children. Mid-life also brought menopause and challenging questions about choices made early in life about mate or career. So, it appears that the time of midlife has been extended to 75 with a chance to recreate yourself once again with verve, confidence and maturity. Just as each stage of life brings new learning and coping skills, this time of life has lessons to learn and challenges to conquer.

The realization may come that you can take a pro-active stance to this time of drastic change that is occurring. Such an impetus to take life by force may come when life becomes boring and same old, same old is not enough. A sudden change, illness or divorce may shake you to the core and call you to question everything about the way you live your life. When you realize that your children are treating you in a condescending manner or wanting to make decisions for you, or not asking for advice on important issues, the time has come to reassess your stance toward family and other relationships. A-ha moments may come to you I experienced one recently. My grand-daughter was being honored by a black-tie event and I was getting 'gussied up' to attend. I had a formal dress but no appropriate shoes. One of my young friends had on some gold high heels that were perfect. She and another friend immediately started chiding me, "You can't wear heels, you will fall and break something." I quickly retorted, "Quit treating me like I am old. I'll wear heels if I want to." This assertion of my agency made me feel so good. This is the time to take back your life and with a new sense of power.

The purpose of this book is to raise consciousness about the opportunities of the middle years as the women's movement did about women's issues beginning in the 1960s, when Betty Friedan's book, the Feminine Mystique, broke into the world and changed women's ideas about their role in society. Their gifts, which were being unrecognized, were allowed to bloom and the Women's Movement began. In 1993, Betty Friedan authored another seminal book called The Fountain of Age, with the hope that it would launch social change the way The Feminine Mystique did. A movement did not begin as a result of this work; maybe the time was not right 20 years ago. Maybe the time is now, perhaps, "This is the time and we are the people."

At whatever age you are reading this book you can begin to question, to take a second look. When you are ready you will want to enter this conversation, and by your attitude and your actions you may become a model for this new stage of life that Boomers are called to create.

I am anxious to know your thought as you experiment with the exercises and suggestions in this book. Did they open your mind to new possibilities? Did they open your heart to accept that challenge that has haunted you for years?

Perhaps the time is now to claim the promise of an abundant life to the end of life. After all, Baby Boomers have created a new and different world of the internet, of space travel, of biotics, of breakthroughs in medicine, of amazing discoveries in science, and every realm of learning. Why stop now?

This boomer generation will accept the challenge to recreate a possible future for all. In order to do this you will have to develop the inner resources of quietude, responding from an open heart, and committing to accepting the challenges of life.

Grow Deep: An example of a man who grew deep and built a movement that changed the mind-set of the generations who have followed him is William Wilberforce. William Wilberforce, English member of Parliament, is widely known for his successful attempt to stop the slave trade and eventually outlaw slavery in England. He is lesser known for his contribution to changing the social mores of his time. At this time, Great Britain ruled the world but the wealthy felt no compassion for the destitute poor and thought the poor were being cursed and the rich had no right to intervene in the Divine order. Therefore, most people lived in abject poverty and misery. Wilberforce, through his faith, saw things very differently and by the force of his personality, his popularity and his wealth, he drew a core group of friends around him who began to model a different way of living in the world and made "doing good fashionable." Wilberforce has been credited with setting a tone of civility that enabled England to avoid the bloodbath and misery of the French Revolution and his leadership has been called one of the most significant accomplishment history.

We who are alive at this time in history can use Wilberforce as our model and choose to tackle the problems that plague our world: hunger; poverty; unemployment; human trafficking; and war. It can become very discouraging to tackle big issues because most of the time, they are enmeshed in even bigger issues. But all we are called on to do is "bloom where we are planted." In the process, we will be joined by allies and together we can effect change to remold the cruelty systems that cause these massive social problem. Social change always begins with empowerment of local people, who begin to see how they can make a difference.

O.K. How many more years do you believe that you have left on this planet? How do you want to invest them, what are you want to live for, what are you willing to die for?

EMERGING FIELD

Websites to explore the topics in the emerging field of dynamic aging :

1. National Center for Creative Aging
   www.creativeaging.org
   415 Albermarie St, NW, Washington, DC
   20016-2105

2. Changing Aging www.changingaging.org
   www.Dr BillThomas.com

3. Fierce With Age, Carol Orsborne

4. Gaea Yudron-www.gaea@sagesplay.org

5. The Radical Age Movement.
   www.theradicalagemovement.com

6. Mary Catherine Bateson author of *Composing a Life Further; The Age of Active Wisdom*

Recent Books that support the conscious aging movement:

1. *Second Journey, Dance of Spirit in Later Life*-Anthony, Bolton-2013. Forty five writers and poets explore the spirit in later life.

2. *The Big Shift: Navigating the New Stage Beyond Mid Life*- Mark Freidman 2011. Co-published with AARP. Freidman is a well-known expert in the field of aging, and has written three books since 1999. His focus is on "encore careers," the concept of finding a new career after retirement.

3. *The Third Chapter, Risk and Adventure in the Twenty*-five years after Fifty-Sara Lawrence Lightfoot. 2008. Dr. Lightfoot, a renowned sociologist, puts forth a challenge that we must develop a compelling vision of later life and not assume that it will be a time of decline. www.fiercewithage.com

4. *Aging in Community*- Janice Blanchard (editor) 2013. This book addresses issues around

housing and offers alternatives to aging in one's own home or institutionalized in a nursing home.

5. *Still Here: Embracing Aging, Changing and Dying.* Ram Dass. 2001. I would put this book on top of the list for people who want to do depth study on spiritual growth whole facing the challenges of aging.

6. *What Should I Do with the Rest of my Life?* Bruce Frankel-2010 A wide range of stories and activities are featured. One man went to Ghana to start a microloan program and retired from a career in government intelligence and decided to become a dancer, even though he had never taken dance. The stories are inspiring and cause the reader to ask himself, "So what should I do with the rest of my life?"

7. *The Force of Character and the Lasting Life-James Hillman-1999.* Hillman postulates that old age is necessary for the human condition and for the maturing of the soul. Hillman's writing is

scholarly and thought provoking and requires a dedicated reader to give the intense concentration necessary to digest it.

The Center for Conscious Eldering:
www.centerforconsciouseldering.com

8. *The Five Stages of the Soul*- Harry R. Moody and David Carroll-1997. The authors use the structure of Joseph Campbell's Heroes Journey as the stages of the Soul's journey. I highly recommend this book for mature readers who understand the struggles of the spiritual journey.

Conscious Aging Alliance:
www.consciousagingalliance.org

9. *Audacious Aging*- edited by Stephanie Marohn-2009. This book contains 40 short essays by leading thinkers including, Jean Houston, Lynn McTaggart, Deepak Chopra, speaking of their vision of the later years.

10. *Claiming your Place at the Fire.*-Richard Leider-2004. Leider uses the fire circle as the central

theme as he states that becoming a 'new elder' is spiritual work. His stated aim is to "fan the flames of vital aging."

11. *I Will Not Die and Unlived Life: Reclaiming Purpose and Passion*- Dawn Markova. 2000. This small sweet book takes its title from a poem the author wrote the night her father died. The implication is that her father had lived an unfulfilled life following the culture of his time, the organizational man. I think this book could be a companion book to *Dynamic Aging*.

12. *Conscious Living, Conscious Aging: Embrace and Savor Your Next Chapter*-Ron Pevny. 2014. Pevny's book is written for the Boomer generation as he invites them to age consciously as they take an intentional approach to living the years after retirement.

13. *Aging as Spiritual Practice*- Lewis Richmond-2012. Richmond is a Zen Buddhist priest and meditation teacher and his book is a guide to

the cultivation of the inner life around the issues of illness, aging and death. While written from a Buddhist perspective anyone could benefit from reading it.

14. *Falling Upward: A Spirituality for the Two Halves of Life.*- Richard Rohr-2011. Rohr's book talks about the first half of life as a time to find one's own identity and way; the second half is to find meaning. Written by a Franciscan teacher it offers profound insights into the Christian Bible and other religious texts.

15. *The Making of an Elder Culture*-Theodore Roszak-2009. Roszak has written 15 books of cultural commentary and in this latest he challenges the Boomer generation to change the entrepreneurial self-serving and neo-conservative values of present day America. He calls for a "new humane social order based on values."

16. *From Age*-ing to Sage-ing: *A Profound Vision of Growing Older*-Zalman Scachter-Shalomi and

Ronald S. Miller. This book is a classic and led the way in thinking and writing about the last developmental stage of life. He focuses on the art of being in the late years as opposed to the art of doing. He implores the reader to take charge of the life he wants to live and become a spiritual elder.

17. *Composing a Further Life: The Age of Active Wisdom*-Mary Catherine Bateson, Vintage, 2011. Bateson's influential book, *Composing a Life,* was a thought leader in the 1990s, and her newest book is a continuation of the first. She tells the stories of elders who have gone from one career to another whole field of endeavor and found life interesting and exciting.

ABOUT THE AUTHOR

 Joy Sloan Jinks is a native Georgian who is widely known through-out the South for her leadership skills and her speaking ability. Her main avenue of leadership has been in three arenas as a community organizer, a consultant and an entrepreneur.

She received the Governor's Award in the Humanities for her contribution as founder of Swamp Gravy, Georgia's Folk Life play. She served on the Advisory board of Georgia Council for the Arts as appointed by three Governors of the State of Georgia. She is a national consultant for community development through the Arts and Culture and has spoken and given workshops in states ranging from New

Hampshire to Louisiana. She is also recognized as an entrepreneur, founder and president of a gourmet condiment manufacturing company. In recognition of her entrepreneurial activities she was a national finalist in the Avon Women of Enterprise competition and received the Georgia Industrial Developers Award.

She was the founder of four not for profit organizations and served as Chair and Board member. She received the Colquitt/Miller county Chamber of Commerce "Life Time Achievement Award" for her contributions to her community.

Her mission has been to be of service which has been fueled by her love of life-long learning, not only for personal growth but to share with others and to inspire new approaches to current problems. She has traveled to every continent except Antarctica and spoken in Kenya, Canada and Scotland. She has studied under renowned teachers such as Jean Houston. She has trained with the Institute of Cultural Affairs to volunteer in Peru, Brazil, India, Kenya and Jamaica. Every experience had added to her skill base and been used to develop programs and organizations which empower local people and enable creative social change.

This is evident in her first book *Dynamic Aging*. After a long and interesting life, she has enlarged her interest and sphere of influence to speak to those who are retiring and to challenge them to change the cultural paradigm about the years following retirement. She has the experience, knowledge and skill to be a leader in the movement that will impact all social and psychological barriers to enjoyment of a dynamic life at any age.

She and her husband live in Colquitt, GA. have three children, eight grandchildren and two great grandchildren.

Joy invites comments and dialogue from her readers. Please contact Joy at:

Website: www.joyjinks.com;

Facebook: https://www.facebook.com/joy.jinks?fref=ts;

Email: joy.jinks@swampgravy.com

Made in the USA
Charleston, SC
23 August 2016